Our relationship to God, like any interpersonal relation-ship, must have communication to be alive and healthy. In *Questions Christians Ask About Prayer and Interces-sion,* Barry Wood shows you how to develop a genuine desire to talk to God. He offers instruction from the plain teachings of God's Word to help you pray effectively and minister to others through intercessory prayer. His care-ful explanation of Scripture reveals how you can have power through answered prayer. This informative and motivating book gives detailed discussion on these and other subjects:

- *praying with power and confidence*
- *spiritual warfare and our armor and weapons*
- *binding and loosing with the keys of the kingdom*
- *unanswered prayer and the will of God*
- *fasting and prayer*
- *prayer and evangelism*
- *how disobedience hinders prayer's effectiveness*
- *the ministry of intercession*
- *why we pray in Jesus' name*
- *how forgiveness affects prayer*

By Barry Wood

Questions New Christians Ask
Questions Non-Christians Ask
Questions Teenagers Ask About Dating and Sex
Questions Christians Ask About Prayer and Intercession

Questions Christians Ask About Prayer and Intercession

Barry Wood

Power Books

Fleming H. Revell Company
Old Tappan, New Jersey

Library of Congress Cataloging in Publication Data

Wood, Barry, date.
    Questions Christians ask about prayer and intercession.

    "Power books."
    Bibliography: p.
    1. Prayer. I. Title.
BV210.2.W66 1984   248.3′2   84-13391
ISBN 0-8007-5177-9

With heartfelt appreciation, this
book is dedicated to those precious
saints God has brought into my life
through the years. Especially those,
who, by their example, have taught me
to pray. Most especially, I am
grateful to our wonderful High Priest,
who is at this very moment interceding
for us.

Contents

Introduction
Lord, Teach Us to Pray

Praying is the most difficult thing we ever learn to do as Christians. Prayer is hard work. It is trench warfare. Now, you may think praying is easy, even a joy. Indeed this can be true. However, real praying, praying that reaches God and moves His heart to answer, is not easy!

I think perhaps the disciples of Jesus thought prayer was easy, until they spent time with Jesus and observed His prayer life. Having watched the Master agonize with the Father, they cried out, "Lord, teach us to pray like that!" (Luke 11:1 paraphrase). These Jewish men, who had been taught all their lives how to pray, now came to the conclusion that there was more to talking with God than they had realized.

As I have traveled America, speaking in many hundreds of churches and observing the life-style of American Christianity (as well as Western Europe), I am convinced that real praying is a lost art. We have forgotten how to pray. This prayerlessness explains much of our powerlessness with God. This is true because our prayer life is our lifeline to a living God. A believer who doesn't have prayer power doesn't have God power. Robert M'Cheyne once said, "What a man is in his prayer closet, that's what the man really is." I agree completely. The test of a believer's walk with God is his talk with God. The church of today is busy with preaching, teaching, conferences, seminars, and every other activity the mind can conceive. We are doing many good things, but not the one essential thing— praying!

This book is designed to accomplish two goals: to teach us to pray and to motivate us to the ministry of effectual, fervent prayer. Do you know how to pray effectively? Do you sense you have power with God through answered prayer? If not, this book is for you. Stay with me, and we'll walk through this challenge together. We'll cry out with the disciples of old, "Lord Jesus, teach us to pray."

What Is Prayer?   Simply put, praying is talking to God. It is the speaking part of our relationship with our Heavenly Father. Christianity is, first and foremost, a personal relationship between an ordinary sinner and an extraordinary God. Like all interpersonal relationships, it must have a speaking part to it. Prayer is that speaking relationship. If the relationship is healthy and alive, there will be real, vital communication. God is our Father; we are His children. Our family life is in trouble if we don't talk.

Why Should We Pray?   Again, we're starting with basics. You should pray to God regularly, daily, because it reflects a healthy relationship. There should be in every believer's heart a genuine desire to talk to God. When there is life, there is evidence of life, such as hunger, activity, and desire. Do you desire to talk to God? If your relationship is good, the desire will be there. Later we will discuss how sin and rebellion destroy our prayer life.

Second, we should pray because the Lord Jesus commanded us to pray. "Now He was telling them a parable to show that at all times they ought to pray and not to lose heart" (Luke 18:1). He knows how much we need to pray. We will "lose heart" if we do not pray "at all times." We must keep in touch with our Father in order to be what He wants us to be. Praying is an act of desire, but it is also an act of obedience. We are to pray even when we don't feel like it.

Third, praying is characteristic of a healthy Christian experience. We are to be like Jesus. He was continually abiding in the Father through prayer. We are to abide in Him and in His Word so that our prayers will be answered (John 15:7). God needs our prayers, because the world needs the answers God gives to our petitions.

Fourth, praying opens the door to supernatural power within our lives. Our prayer can put the Lord Jesus to work in our world. In a later chapter, we'll want to see how praying with power allows God to do work He ordinarily would not do. This book is offered with the hope that thousands can be taught about prayer power and then put it to work.

Questions and Answers. We all have questions about the "deeper things" of the Word of God, so we'll seek to faithfully explore these truths together. They fit into three general categories: prayer, spiritual warfare, and intercession.

My prayer for you, the reader, is that Jesus Himself shall take you into the Holy of Holies with Him in prayer and intercession.

Questions Christians Ask
About Prayer and Intercession

Chapter 1

Prayer is a conversation between an ordinary human being and an extraordinary God, often about very ordinary things.

1

How to Live Miraculously

Can I Really Get Supernatural Results in Prayer?

Most of us feel at times that church, religion, and our faith are a drag, a bore, or at least ineffective to produce real change in our world. We could all use a miracle every now and then. If only we could walk with Jesus like the disciples in years gone by. How exciting that would be!

Miracles Promised

Well, hold on tight, because I want God to show you His secrets to miraculous living. In John's gospel, we have a tremendous promise from the Lord Jesus. "Truly, truly, I say to you, he who believes in Me, the works that I do shall he do also; and greater works than these shall he do; because I go to the Father" (John 14:12). Now there is a startling promise. Jesus says every true believer should do two miraculous things:

1. Equal Christ's ministry—"The works that I do shall he do also. . . ."

2. Exceed Christ's ministry—"and greater works than these shall he do; because I go to the Father."

Amazing! How in the world can the average Christian ever hope to *exceed* the works of Jesus? Such a promise seems

17

ridiculous. Obviously, Jesus had something wonderful in mind, but what, and how?

Two Keys to Miraculous Living.   Yes, our Lord did intend for us to equal and exceed His ministry. He also told us how this could be accomplished. In this great fourteenth chapter of John, Jesus teaches us two keys to miraculous living after He is gone from this earth: He teaches about prayer in His name, and He teaches about the coming of the Holy Spirit to indwell the believer.

It is also obvious that He meant for the promise of verse twelve (to equal and exceed) to be accomplished by what He said in verses thirteen and fourteen: "And whatever you ask in My name, that will I do, that the Father may be glorified in the Son. If you ask Me anything in My name, I will do it." The promise of verse twelve is to be fulfilled by the "asking" in verses thirteen and fourteen. Did you catch the significance of this truth? Prayer in Jesus' name is a key that unlocks the door to miracles in your life. Yes, prayer! The most common experience can be a key to miracles.

Jesus also continues in verses fifteen and following to talk about the Holy Spirit to empower the believer. The Holy Spirit indwells us to give content and faith to our prayers. Therefore, we have the equipment we need to unlock heaven's treasure chest.

Why No Miracles.   The question arises: then why do we not see more of the supernatural in the church or in individual lives? Amazingly, I have found that *most* Christians are ignorant of these truths. Somehow, the message has not gotten through to the masses. Yet it is no secret that Jesus tells us only to "ask anything" in His name and He will do it. It seems that if we know how to ask, He is willing to perform in our behalf. Thus, when a believing child asks the Father in Jesus' name, then Jesus Himself goes to work, continuing His miraculous ministry. The more of us who pray, the more ministry He performs.

Look at it this way: you make a need known to God the Father. Then, God the Father turns to God the Son and tells Him to go meet your need. Jesus gets up off the throne and goes to meet your need. You ask and the Father sends the Son. What a concept. What a promise! My prayers put Jesus to work.

In the chapters that follow, we shall seek to understand some of the elements of this miracle of praying in Jesus' name. Why pray in Jesus' name? What about the will of God in prayer? Does the Holy Spirit help us to pray? These questions we will answer, but for now we must believe that we can touch the throne of the universe and that our prayers can change the nature of things here on earth.

Chapter 2

The biggest thing God ever did for me was to teach me to pray in the Holy Spirit. We are never really men of prayer in the best sense, until we are filled with the Holy Ghost. Therefore, Lord, teach us to pray in the Spirit.

Samuel Chadwick
The Path of Prayer

2

How to Pray in the Holy Spirit

What Is Praying in the Holy Spirit?

Have you ever prayed "in the Spirit?" Regrettably, most Christians have no idea what this means. Others fear this is some "charismatic" extreme and shy away. Yet Scripture commands us to pray "in the Spirit." Paul urges us to "pray at all times in the Spirit" (Ephesians 6:18). The Holy Spirit earnestly desires to help us in our praying. This is why our Lord Christ, in John 14, tells us there are two keys to supernatural living: prayer and the Holy Spirit. We must learn to allow the Holy Spirit to become vitally involved in our communications with God the Father.

Praying in the Spirit is described graphically in Romans: "And in the same way the Spirit also helps our weakness; for we do not know how to pray as we should, but the Spirit Himself intercedes for us with groanings too deep for words; and He who searches the hearts knows what the mind of the Spirit is, because He intercedes for the saints according to the will of God" (Romans 8:26, 27). Notice, in praying, the Holy Spirit *Himself* desires to intercede for us. Why is this true? Because the Holy Spirit's very nature demands that He help us. He is the "Spirit of grace and of supplication" (Zechariah 12:10). The Holy Spirit is our helper in prayer, and praying *must* include His presence and power. Indeed, Jude 20 commands us to be "building yourselves up on your most holy faith; praying in the Holy Spirit."

When Are You Really Praying?

In a sentence, real praying is praying in the Holy Spirit. Other "praying" isn't true praying at all. It is only religious activity. It has no genuine effect on God or the one praying. This is why much public praying is only religious ceremony, meaningless and monotonous! What a contrast is praying in the Spirit. It is prayer that is energized, empowered, quickened, and sustained by the Spirit of God Himself!

Why are we so surprised that the Holy Spirit should control our praying? We expect Him to empower our preaching, our witnessing, and our worship. Why not our praying? I am convinced that the acid test of our walk with God is not our preaching, giving, doing, or attending; but rather our power in praying. Prayer is the barometer of our power with God. Does God talk to you? Does He listen and answer when you speak to Him? More than this, does He personally energize, empower, quicken, and sustain your talks with Him? This is the real test of godliness.

Praying "With" the Spirit.   Scripture speaks of praying "with" the Spirit as well as praying "in" the Spirit. These two experiences are not the same. In 1 Corinthians 14:14, 15, the apostle Paul describes praying "with the Spirit." This is not a reference to the Holy Spirit of God, but rather he is referring to your human spirit. Praying with the spirit is praying with an unknown tongue, wherein the mind doesn't understand what is being said. Many today call this praying in a "prayer language"; however, praying in the Spirit is a whole different thing. We are not commanded to pray in tongues, but we are commanded to "pray at all times *in the Spirit*" (Ephesians 6:18, emphasis added). Praying in the Spirit is not a "charismatic" experience for a few select folks who belong to a special group or denomination who call themselves charismatic or Pentecostal. Praying in the Spirit is prayer, real prayer. It is for everyone.

Guaranteed Answers

Have you ever prayed to God and really needed assurance that the answer would come? Or have you ever doubted whether you were praying according to God's will? What is the cause for such doubts in your prayer requests? Prayer in the Holy Spirit will guarantee your prayers are according to God's will, because God's Spirit will be giving you the content to your prayers. Note this truth: only a prayer prayed in the Holy Spirit will always be according to the will of God and thus assured a ready reply.

When a Lost Man Prays.   The leader of a major denomination raised quite a controversy a few years ago when, in a press interview, he declared that God would not answer the prayer of a Jewish rabbi because he does not accept Jesus Christ as Savior and Messiah. Now, many critical voices were raised in chorus against this religious leader. He was assailed as a bigot. Was he? That probably depends upon your view of Scripture. If one takes Scripture as seriously as I do, then we are led to some interesting conclusions about prayer and unbelievers. Jesus teaches us to pray in *His* name, not Yahweh or Allah, or some other deity. He is our mediator to God. We come in His name. The Holy Spirit honors the name of the Lord Jesus. Therefore, a lost man cannot pray in the Spirit, because he does not have the Holy Spirit living in Him. He is "devoid of the Spirit" (Jude 19). It is my conclusion that God only answers a lost man's prayers if and when He knows that the answer will move that person toward salvation in Jesus Christ. Acts 10 illustrates this in the experience of the Roman centurian, Cornelius. Scripture describes him as "a devout man, and one who feared

God ... and prayed to God continually" (Acts 10:2). Again, in verse 31, we are told that God heard the prayers of Cornelius and answered them! So, God does answer some pagan prayers. However, He only answers those that will lead a lost man to the Savior Jesus Christ.

Strong Assurance. How blessed is the born-again believer! God's Spirit indwells him and desires to pray through him to assure his answered prayers. Let's turn our attention once again to Romans 8:26, 27, to learn more about this praying in the Holy Spirit. Paul says we "... do not know how to pray as we should ..." (Romans 8:26). This is true of every believer. You and I start to pray, and before much time passes, we do not know what to say to our great God. Often we say the wrong things, praying "amiss," as James 4:3 (KJV) says. At times, I've had to thank God for unanswered prayer, because I was praying for the wrong things from impure motives.

Our Helplessness in Praying

Romans 8:26 reveals to us that we are so helpless in our praying that "we do not know how to pray as we should." Why are we unable to pray as we should? Notice that the Holy Spirit helps our "weakness" (Romans 8:26). The word *weakness* is in the singular, not plural. It's not that we have many weaknesses or shortcomings in our prayer life, even though we do have many weaknesses; actually, we have one great weakness. It affects every area of our lives, not just prayer. It is the weakness of the flesh. Our fallen nature, damaged by sin and self, is our crippling weakness. In the "flesh," we cannot please God (Romans 8:8). In other words, in our own strength, we cannot "perform" spiritual acts that impress or please God. Think of it: preaching, praying, witnessing, giving, serving that are done in our own strength cannot please God. This is our "weakness," our infirmity. I once heard this weakness stated as a spiritual axiom. It is an axiom that we must live by. Our weakness is "our total inability to do anything in the spiritual realm in our own flesh."

This is why the Holy Spirit must help us. He must indwell us, fill us, control us, and live His life through us. When you and I come to the place where we realize our total inability to pray, then God has us right where He wants us—dependent on Him. As long as we are trying to help God, He can't help us. Christ Jesus wants to be more than our Savior, He wants to be our life source. In our praying, His Spirit is to be our comforter to heal our infirmity, our strength to replace our weakness.

The Helper in Our Praying. When we cooperate with the Holy Spirit, He can prompt us to pray and put the desire in us. If we lack the desire to pray, we need to get right with Him. Out of His Lordship over us comes the desire to pray. When the Holy Spirit is controlling us, we'll want to pray and to do it frequently.

Also, He will give us the content (words) of our prayer. Praying in the Holy Spirit means that the Spirit Himself actually does the praying and makes intercession through us. Using your mind and personality, the Spirit prays through you to the Father. That's supernatural praying. Now, do you believe this is possible? Does this sound "way out" to you? It shouldn't sound strange. You believe the Holy Spirit can speak through other areas of the Christian life:

> when preaching—God can preach through a man;
> when teaching—God can teach through a man;
> when living—God can live through a man.

Why not when praying? Cannot God pray through a man? Yes, He can. More than that, He greatly desires to do so. Romans 8:26 says He "groans" in us, so great is His desire to supplicate through the prayers of a believer.

Groanings of the Spirit. These "groanings" are not always human words. They often are just the Spirit of Jesus in you, desiring fellowship with you. These groanings are just a burden or a divine impulse. Often there are no words; the Spirit is just wanting us to commune with Him. How precious is our God to desire to share Himself with our sinful humanness. Too often, we speak rote prayers when we should be still and know that He is God!

Praying According to God's Will

There is one other thought in Paul's teaching in Romans 8:27: "He intercedes ... according to the will of God." How can you guarantee that your requests will be answered? It's really very simple: always pray in the Holy Spirit. The Holy Spirit always prays according to God's will and every prayer uttered according to God's will shall be answered with a resounding "Yes." First John 5:14 promises, "And this is the confidence which we have before Him, that, if we ask anything according to His will, He hears us." Pray in the Spirit and you'll get answers!

Praying for Healing. Suppose someone asks you to pray for healing,[1] but you don't know if it's God's will to heal that person! What we usually pray is, "God, if it be Your will, heal this person." That's our escape clause. We put in a theological "if" to protect us. It takes no faith to pray an "if" prayer. This kind of praying does not constitute real praying. It's when we do not know the revealed will of God that we can pray for the Holy Spirit to help us.

When We Pray. Some practical guidelines would be helpful at this point. There are some steps of discipline which can allow God's Spirit to energize your praying before you pray:

1. *Confess every known sin.* Isaiah 59:2 tells us that, "your iniquities have made a separation between you and your God, and your sins have hidden His face from you, so that He does not hear."

2. *Choose against self.* Submit yourself to God and His will. Declare Jesus as Lord of all. Just as you begin your prayer time confessing sin, you should tell God, "Jesus is Lord of my Life; Lord Jesus, I'm Yours." This verbal confession confirms a commitment in your heart and thrills the heart of God.

3. *Commit your prayer time to the Holy Spirit.* Verbally plead your helplessness. Invite Him to pray through you. Ask Him to control your devotions.

4. *Wait on the Lord.* "Be still and know that I am God," Scripture says. Now wait quietly or read the Word out loud. God's Spirit will begin to commune with you. You may get an impression, a thought. Pray it verbally to God. You have every right to believe those thoughts are from God.

5. *Ask, Is it me or God?* You might wonder, "I don't know if the impressions that come are mine or the Lord's." Why does there have to be a difference between what you want and what God wants? If you have just declared Jesus as Lord, confessed every known sin, and asked the Holy Spirit to control your thoughts, then *your* thoughts and *God's* thoughts will be the same! Psalms 37:4 urges, "Delight yourself in the Lord; And He will give you the desires of your heart."

Praying When You Are Uncertain. Knowing God's will is not always easy.[2] At times, we must follow some guidelines in prayer:

- Pray until you get an answer.

- Pray until you get the assurance of an answer.

- Pray until God says "no."

You may question how God speaks in these situations. He does so through His indwelling Spirit. Scripture commands us

to "let the peace of Christ rule in your hearts ..." (Colossians
3:15). How can you have peace in your heart about a request
you've made? God's Spirit will grant this peace when He is allowed to "rule" in our hearts. The word *rule* that Paul uses here
is unique. It is one of six Greek words translated as "rule" in
the New Testament. It means to "act as umpire."[3] Thus, God's
Spirit will be our referee, umpire, or arbitrator in these times of
uncertainty. Therefore, pray without ceasing; He will give you
peace!

Promised Answers. Praying for those things God has already
promised to provide in Holy Scripture is a different proposi-
tion. The same Spirit that is in you also wrote the book He inspired. Claiming Bible promises is an act of faith. I suggest you
pray—

- *Reminding God of His promise.*
  Quote His Word right back to Him.

- *Bringing the need before Him.*
  "Tell God your needs and don't forget to thank Him for
  His answers" (Philippians 4:6 TLB).

- *Claiming the answer by faith.*
  Jesus promised that "all things for which you pray and
  ask, believe that you have received them, and they shall
  be granted you" (Mark 11:24).

- *Praising Him continually, believing the answer is on the
  way.*
  It is at this point we act as though we already have the
  answer. We then leave the When, Where, and How up
  to our Great God, knowing, "they shall be granted
  you."

In the following chapters, we will seek to develop further our
understanding of the miraculous power of prayer.

Resources

1. In a previous book, I discuss healing and prayer in detail. See chapter 7 of *Questions New Christians Ask* (Old Tappan, New Jersey: Fleming H. Revell Company, 1979), pp. 76–86.

2. See chapter 1, "How to Know God's Will," in *Questions New Christians Ask*.

3. The word is *brabeuō*. See W. E. Vine, *Expository Dictionary of Old and New Testament Words* (Old Tappan, New Jersey: Fleming H. Revell Company, 1981), p. 307.

Chapter 3

The two key elements in authoritative praying is to know who He *is to whom you pray and, second, to know who* you are *in Him. "I pray that the eyes of your heart may be enlightened" (Ephesians 1:18).*

3
How to Pray With Power

Why Do I Not Have Confidence in Prayer?

Why does God not answer my prayers? Have you ever voiced this question? Of course you have. Who hasn't at one time or another? There are a number of reasons why God says "no," and I've dealt with them in a previous book;[1] however, any believer can pray with the confidence that God will answer. Every believer *should* pray with boldness. Hebrews encourages us to "draw near with confidence to the throne of grace, that we may receive mercy and may find grace to help in time of need" (Hebrews 4:16).

Knowing Who You Are

Confidence in prayer is the result of several factors. One of those key factors is faith. The prayer of faith will be the topic of the next chapter. Even more important than having faith in God is knowing who you are in Christ. Identification with Christ is what gives us the courage and confidence to ask boldly before the throne of a Holy God. Only a child of God who knows his or her position in Christ can ever hope to pray with authority. Yet it seems so few modern-day Christians fully understand what our identification with Christ really means. Boldness in prayer arises from the true knowledge of who God is and how He feels about you, His child.

The Authority of the Believer.   You see, every child of God has "Throne Rights." These throne rights are a result of what the Lord Jesus did for us on the cross. The believer's throne rights are his authority in Christ Jesus. Paul the apostle describes our authority in Ephesians 1:18–23:

> I pray that the eyes of your heart may be enlightened, so that you may know what is the hope of His calling, what are the riches of the glory of His inheritance in the saints, and what is the surpassing greatness of His power toward us who believe. These are in accordance with the working of the strength of His might which He brought about in Christ, when He raised Him from the dead, and seated Him at His right hand in the heavenly places, far above all rule and authority and power and dominion, and every name that is named, not only in this age, but also in the one to come. And He put all things in subjection under His feet, and gave Him as head over all things to the church, which is His body, the fulness of Him who fills all in all.

This passage is really a prayer. Paul prays that the eyes of your heart may be enlightened, so that you may know who you are in Christ. This paragraph is a very definitive passage revealing our throne rights. We are heirs through Christ. We have an inheritance (*see* Romans 8:17) which was purchased for us through the completed work of Christ in His life, death, burial, resurrection, and ascension.

The Seat of Our Authority.   "Which He brought about in Christ, when He raised Him from the dead, and seated Him at His right hand in the heavenly places" (Ephesians 1:20). These words tell us that Christ has risen to the throne of God. He is ruling the universe. This we all know, but did you know that you are ruling with Him in those same "heavenly places"? Paul affirms this in more detail in two other passages: "and raised us up with Him, and seated us with Him in the heavenly places, in Christ Jesus" (Ephesians 2:6); "and in Him you have been made complete, and He is the head over all rule and authority" (Colossians 2:10).

What a statement! We (all born-again believers) are seated *"with Him";* we share in His victory. We are coheirs of His rule and power. We are "complete" in Him. Thus, everything that is true of our Lord's victory of the world, the flesh, and the devil, is also true of the believer. We are at this moment "seated" with Him in heavenly places. That is your eternal address—seated on the throne. Not seated when you die, or when Jesus comes again for His church. You are there now, ruling and reigning with Christ far above all rule and authority and power (*see* Ephesians 1:21). All of the power of God that is given to Christ Jesus is also given to the church, "which is His body, the fulness of Him who fills all in all" (Ephesians 1:23).

Positional Truth. These truths are what we call "positional" truths. In other words, God sees the church as complete in Christ. From God's perspective, we have already made our enemies our footstool. God sees us as already in heaven with Him. We do not stand before a Holy God in a position of condemnation as guilty sinners, but we stand in a position of forgiveness, exaltation, and as coheirs with Christ. God loves us through His Son. We are "in Christ" in our position before God.

Position and Prayer. You may wonder what this has to do with boldness in prayer. Everything! How can you approach the throne of a Holy God with the guilt of sin before your eyes? The apostle John states it well, "Beloved, if our heart does not condemn us, we have confidence before God" (1 John 3:21). Does your heart often condemn you? Does guilt, failure, or lack of confidence keep you from praying and asking? Friend, this is Satan's trick to condemn your heart. He puts you on a "performance" basis rather than a "positional" basis before God. In our performance, none is worthy before God. However, in Christ, we are all encouraged to come boldly to the throne of Grace to find help in the time of need. As children of God, we are loved and accepted. We are not beggars coming to God's back door, begging for scraps. We are rich in Christ, heirs with Him. We ask and receive, because of what He has done and who we are in Him!

The Source of Our Authority

Returning to Paul's prayer in Ephesians 1, he wants us to realize that this great inheritance and power to rule over every name that is named in this age or the age to come (the spiritual world) is given "toward us who believe" (Ephesians 1:19). Our faith in this revealed truth is the key to our boldness before God. God's great power is toward those who believe. Are you a believer? Not just a doctrinal believer of theology, but an experiential believer. Notice Paul prays that the "eyes of your heart" be enlightened. Not the eyes of reason, or the mind, but the eyes of your heart. You see, these truths of our position in Christ are not understood with the rational mind. They are revealed by the Holy Spirit to *your* spirit. Only the heart can perceive this profound truth. It is for those who *believe*. It is beyond reason, but not beyond faith. Faith is our source of power and authority with God. He has done His complete work in Christ. Now we must believe what He has accomplished is for us. I have personally seen the power of God released through prayer when a believer truly knows in his heart who he is in Christ. All of heaven is at his disposal. A believing saint on his knees is a force to be dealt with.

Mountain Movers. This prayer of faith is what Jesus had in mind when He said, "Truly I say to you, whoever says to this mountain, 'Be taken up and cast into the sea,' and does not doubt in his heart, but believes that what he says is going to happen, it shall be granted him. Therefore I say to you, all things for which you pray and ask, believe that you have received them, and they shall be granted you" (Mark 11:23, 24).

What a wonderful promise! Have you got any "mountains" that stand in your way? A "mountain" represents any obstacle that stands between you and the will of God. It may be the devil himself. Jesus says we have the power to remove *any* obstacle just by speaking our faith. We speak to mountains and they move! That's authority, that's real power. I told you, we have a direct line to the throne room!

Moses and Joshua. A great illustration of mountain-moving prayer and intercession is found in the experience of Moses and Joshua as they encounter King Amalek and the tribe of Amalekites. God has told Moses to possess the land of Canaan; however, there are obstacles in the way. Amalek is a fierce pagan king. Moses and Joshua must drive him out. What does Moses do? He has a twofold battle plan. He will fight for God on two fronts—the physical and the spiritual. Joshua will go down to meet the army of Amalek. He will fight in the physical realm. Moses goes up on the mountaintop to pray. Exodus 17 records this strange battle plan, "So Moses said to Joshua, 'Choose men for us, and go out, fight against Amalek. Tomorrow I will station myself on the top of the hill with the staff of God in my hand.' And Joshua did as Moses told him, and fought against Amalek; and Moses, Aaron, and Hur went up to the top of the hill" (Exodus 17:9, 10).

Now, if I had been Captain Joshua, I would have been inclined to argue with General Moses! I would have recommended that Moses go down and fight Amalek and I stay on the mountain and pray. That certainly sounds safer!

Staff and Swords. Notice: two battles, two enemies, two different kinds of weapons. Joshua fights Amalek with swords and spears, but Amalek is not the real enemy; Satan is the real enemy. Amalek is only Satan's servant. "For our struggle is not against flesh and blood, but against the rulers, against the powers, against the world forces of this darkness, against the spiritual forces of wickedness in the heavenly places" (Ephesians 6:12).

Moses fights the real enemy with spiritual weapons. He is interceding for Joshua. In his hand is the staff (rod) of God. This was once only a common stick used to herd sheep. Now since Moses met God on the mountain, this stick is a "rod of God." This staff is the power of God committed to the hand of a man of faith; in Moses' hand, this stick is the power of God. So, in faith, Moses on the mountain prays against the mountain that stands before the children of Israel: Amalek. When Moses raises the rod and prays, Joshua defeats Amalek; yet when Moses grows weary and his arms drop down and the rod is lowered, Amalek prevails in battle against Joshua. What a fight! What a battle! What a war! Yet it was not being won with swords and spears. It was being won or lost in prayer! That's exactly the way it is in our daily lives. Friend, your enemy is not Amalek (or your boss, husband, or wife). Your enemy is the power behind that person. Too often we've fought the wrong battle, with the wrong enemy, using the wrong weapons, and losing every round!

Using the Rod. I once heard a fellow say, "I wish I had me a stick like Moses had ... I'd beat up on Amalek like Joshua did." Great news: You *have* a rod like Moses! Every Christian has a rod of God. With it you can part the waters, defeat your Amaleks, and claim the promised land. Where is our rod? Listen, you have two rods, not just one. Our two "rods of God" are our position in Christ and our faith in the name of Jesus. Think again, what was the significance of Moses' staff? It was the power of God committed to the hand of a man of faith. God has today committed this power to His church. He gives us two rods: our union with Christ and the name of Jesus. Because of who we are in Christ, God asks us to expect to move mountains. Jesus tells us to ask "in My name."

The Williams translation of Mark 16:17 reads, "And the following signs will attend those who believe: by using My name they will drive out demons." The name of Jesus is the Christian's rod of Moses. By using His name (in faith) we can drive out demons. Each of us has some "demons," or an Amalek that stands in our way. We need to put them out of our way, remove them. We can do as Moses did, using the rod God has given us: the powerful name of Jesus. Our union with Him and our faith in that union give us ultimate authority over the world, the flesh, and the devil. That also gives us access to the Father (*see* Romans 5:2) at any time of the day or night. It is my prayer for you, dear reader, that together we can learn to use the rod and begin to win mighty battles through prayer!

Resources

1. Chapter 9, *Questions New Christians Ask* (Old Tappan, New Jersey: Fleming H. Revell Company, 1979), pp. 93–102.

Chapter 4

Faith is not believing God can,
or that God will, *but real faith
is believing that God* already has.

4

How to Pray in Faith

Why Do I Not Have Enough Faith When I Pray?

Have you ever prayed a prayer, made some large request of God, then as soon as you said "Amen," doubted the answer would come? Perhaps you've said, "He won't answer that prayer." Well, I've done that—to my shame. At times, God has shamed me further by answering the prayer even in the midst of my doubting. He is a sovereign God! However, God does honor the prayer of faith. Faith is the key that unlocks the door to heaven's treasure house. Faith thrills the heart of God. Listen to the promises of Scripture regarding prayer and faith:

And Jesus answered saying to them, "Have faith in God. Truly I say to you, whoever says to this mountain, 'Be taken up and cast into the sea,' and does not doubt in his heart, but believes that what he says is going to happen, it shall be granted him. Therefore I say to you, all things for which you pray and ask, believe that you have received them, and they shall be granted you."

Mark 11:22–24

Faith Pleases God

Because God is our Father, it pleases Him for us to trust Him. He loves for us to take Him at His word. Nothing pleases Him quite as much as simple, childlike faith. Hebrews says, "without faith it is impossible to please Him" (Hebrews 11:6).

This is especially true when we approach Him in prayer. Our Lord stressed this so strongly in Mark 11:22–24. He commands us to have faith in God. He urges us to pray believing so we can *already have* the requests we make. These statements tell us something of the nature of God. He desires to give to His believing children![1]

Begging, Shouting, Apologizing.   Jesus tells us simply to come to God and ask, seek, knock (Luke 11:9, 10). Do you come to pray with the simple trust of a child who knows his father's love and goodness? Many people I know approach the throne with attitudes that are quite the opposite of faith and trust.

- *The Beggar.*   Here's one man who comes to God like a beggar. He pleads, begs, coaxes, urges, trying to "pry" a blessing out of the clenched fist of a stubborn God. This man, even though he may be a Christian, doesn't know who he is in Christ, nor does he really know who God is. He is fearful of God, so he is a beggar, pleading. I tell you, this attitude is not what our Lord teaches, nor does it honor the cross of the Lord Jesus. It saddens the heart of God.

- *The Shouter.*   Here's a person who thinks God is hard of hearing! Speak loudly or God won't hear or answer. He thinks he must shout at God in prayer. You've heard this guy in church—without a microphone! In John 14:14, Jesus said, "Ask Me anything and I will do it" (paraphrase). Notice He said, "Ask Me," not "shout at Me." You and I do not need to raise our voices to God. He knows the thoughts and intentions of the heart. In contrite heart and simple faith, we "ask."

- *The Apologizer.* Here's another pathetic saint, who thinks every approach to God should begin with an apology. "Well, God, here I am again. Yeah, it's me, the original screw-up!" This poor fellow wears sackcloth and ashes to church and has a cloud of doom over his head for a halo. His favorite invocation is "Woe is me!" Now, guilt can be very real, and it is a terrible thing. Guilt is a thief that robs us of all joy in the Lord. In my book *Questions New Christians Ask,*[2] we have discussed the fact that the Christian does not stand before a Holy God guilty and condemned. Even the defeated, carnal Christian is not excluded from God's presence (perhaps excluded from His *pleasure,* but never His presence).

The Believer. When approaching God's presence in prayer, our disposition is not to be that of a beggar, shouter, or an apologizer, but rather that of a confident believer. We do have access to God. Romans 5:2 states it well: "By whom also we have access by faith into this grace wherein we stand..." (KJV).

There are two things about this verse that excite me. First is the word *access.* It means an "introduction," like an introduction into the presence of royalty. It means a letter of recommendation, a carte blanche. In Christ, we also have "access," direct access into the throne room of the King of the universe. In Him, we have a passport which introduces us as worthy, because of our blood-bought relationship in Christ.

Second, Paul says we "have access." The verb *have* is in the perfect tense rather than the more common present tense, the emphasis being that we have eternally complete access to God which can never be changed or revoked. We continually stand in grace, loved by God forever! Marvelous truth to live by! Thus, when we come to pray, we are to believe we are welcome in His presence.

> Thou art coming to a king,
> Large petitions with thee bring;
> His grace and power are such,
> You can never ask too much.

Differing Kinds of Faith

Not Just Wishing. Because faith pleases God so much and allows Him to work in our lives, it is extremely important that we know what faith is and how it works. *Faith* is a term that means different things to different people. What is important is to know what *God* means by "faith." A good learning tool is to state what a thing is not. Faith is not wishing or hoping. Nor is it to be confused with the power of positive thinking. Biblical faith is not just faith in faith. It is faith in God!

People often will say, "God can do anything," and call this faith. Of course God can do anything, but it doesn't take much faith to believe that. You cannot get to heaven on that kind of faith. What if the thief on the cross next to Jesus had said, "Jesus can save me." Would that have saved him? No, it would not have. There is no trust involved, no asking to be received, or dependence on God.

Others have the "God will" kind of faith. This is better than the "God can" kind of faith, because this person says, "God will meet my needs. God will save me from my sins some day." However, a man cannot get to heaven on this presumptuous kind of idea. To believe God will do something is not the same as asking and claiming in faith that He has done it.

Biblical Faith. Real faith is the "God has" met my needs kind of trust. This is the scriptural faith spoken of in the great eleventh chapter of Hebrews: "Now faith is the substance of things hoped for, the evidence of things not seen" (Hebrews 11:1 KJV).

Faith is not hoping; faith is having. The word translated "substance," means reality, or real nature of, as it refers in Hebrews 1:3 to Christ being the substance of God Himself. Therefore, if I have faith in a thing hoped for, it becomes a reality in my life. If I believe it, I've got it! Amazing? Yes, but nonetheless true. This is the teaching of Jesus in Mark 11:24: "All things for which you pray and ask, believe that you have received them, and they shall be granted you." The moment I truly believe, the answer is on the way. The language of the original text is so strong that the New American Standard Bible rightly corrects the Authorized Version from "you *shall* receive" to the correct tense, "you *have* received." Thus the moment you truly believe, you have already (past tense) received! I didn't say it—Jesus did! Faith is receiving. Someone defined scriptural faith this way, "Faith is acting like it's so when it's not so, and it shall be so." It's turning things hoped for into reality.

Faith and God's Will. We must not be led astray here. Jesus told us to have "faith in God." That includes God's plan and purpose for your life. He is sovereign, and His will is supreme. All the faith in the world will not change His sovereign will. People with cancer have believed God would heal their sickness, and yet they died. First John 5:14 qualifies this clearly when it says, "if we ask anything according to His will, He hears us." Verse fifteen assures us that when we ask (in faith) according to His will, "we have the requests which we have asked from Him."

My point here is that when we know the revealed will of God as clearly stated in Scripture, we can claim it as a promise. God always makes provisions *for* us before He makes promises *to* us. We can live or die by the promises of God. Prayer is simply turning God's promises into daily provisions.

I'm Untouchable! Recently I spent two weeks in the Socialist Republic of Romania. Everywhere we went we were followed by the secret police. The pastors, with whom I was working, live under continual threat to their safety. I asked one of these courageous men how he could sleep at night. Did he not fear for his life? With an angelic smile, he replied, "I'm untouchable. As long as God has work for me to do, the police cannot harm me." Tears filled my eyes. I was made to feel both shame and pride. I thought of David's words, "The Lord is my light and my salvation; whom shall I fear? The Lord is the defense of my life; whom shall I dread?" (Psalms 27:1). This dear man of God was like Daniel in the lions' den, but his heart was not troubled, because God had promised to close the mouths of the lions. We need to remember this when we pray. Anything God has promised in His word, we should claim as our provision. Faith is simply taking God at His word and expecting Him to do what He says He will do.

Faith Is Seeing

In your life, there are things you hope for, wish for, or dream about. How can you make your dreams come true? First, remove those things that are not God's will but only your selfish desires. Second, can you believe a simple promise like Philippians 4:19: "And my God shall supply all your needs according to His riches in glory in Christ Jesus"? Okay, sort out your needs from your wants. God hasn't promised to give me all my wants; He *has* promised to meet my needs. Hebrews says faith is "the evidence of things not seen." Suppose you have a need, a real and genuine need. How can you "see" the evidence of this hoped-for need being provided? Well, let me give you an example.

Out of the Blue. Years ago, when I was a freshman in college, I began to see God's miraculous provision. The rent was due on my apartment; I was broke, and my roommate was broke. Where was the rent going to come from? We were nearly a month behind. We finally gave up trying to figure out how to earn this money and, as a last resort, began to pray for it. I was nineteen years old, a young would-be preacher seeking the rent from my Heavenly Father!

That very week, I got a letter from the United States Forestry Service in which was a check for the rent! Well, not for the rent, but it was for me! The previous summer, I had been "drafted" one day to fight a forest fire in Oregon. We had worked all day and night fighting that blaze. What I didn't know at the time was that the government *pays* you for fire fighting! So, months later, here comes a check in the mail, the very week I prayed and asked God to meet a very real need!

My point: faith is seeing the needs you hoped for. When we believe God and ask Him, He is honor-bound to keep His word. Christian friend, we have not because we ask not. Believe and ask so God can provide. Anything we need, we can have if we believe it is already provided.

Seeing Is Believing. There are two groups of people with two kinds of faith. The first group is the "seeing is believing" group. In John 20:25 (KJV), Thomas said, "Except I shall see ... I will not believe." He had to see a resurrected Lord before he would believe in a resurrected Lord. Thomas had sense faith. We say, "Lord, You give me victory, then I'll believe I have it." THAT'S NOT FAITH! That's why Jesus said you've got to believe you've already got it and *then* you'll have it.

Jesus did not compliment Thomas. He said, "Blessed are those who never see, and they don't need to see—they just believe!" (John 20:29, author's paraphrase). That is scriptural faith. We need to move out of the realm of the senses and move into the realm of the Scriptures. Here is where we discover the second kind of faith, which says, "Faith is seeing what I hope for." If I have the conviction that I have already received what God has promised, then I shall SEE what I hoped for! Again, this is saving faith. You didn't see Jesus die and rise from the grave the third day; you just trusted the Word. It was all the evidence you needed. You believed the Word, and then you saw Jesus and experienced His forgiveness. Faith is acting like it is so when it is not so, and it will be so!

A Leper's Faith. Luke, chapter seventeen, describes ten lepers who came to Jesus crying, " 'Jesus, Master, have mercy on us!' And when He saw them, He said to them, 'Go and show yourselves to the priests.' And it came about that as they were going, they were cleansed" (Luke 17:13, 14). A cleansed or healed leper had to go show himself to the priest to be approved that he was really healed. Jesus tells them to go show themselves to the priest *before* they are healed. What if they had said, "Lord, we can't go to the priest—we're not healed yet"? Jesus, in effect, was saying, "Act as though it is when it isn't, and it will be so." They believed and started toward the temple, and ". . . as they were going, they were cleansed. . . . And He said to him, . . . 'Your faith has made you well' " (verses 14 and 19).

Victory and Faith

First John 5:4 equates victory in life with faith in God. "For whatever is born of God overcomes the world; and this is the victory that has overcome the world—our faith." Do you see this fantastic truth? We already have the victory if we have the "God has" kind of faith. Note that the verb "has overcome" is in the perfect tense in the original. It could be translated "and this is the victory that overcame the world, is overcoming the world, and will overcome the world—our faith." Thus, victory is already provided. Faith just appropriated that victory into each day's need. The point is this: You have the victory just by believing that Jesus Christ has already won it (1 John 5:5).

You say, "Do you mean I have the victory over every problem just by believing I have the victory?" That's right! That's exactly right! You say, "I don't believe that!" No, and you don't have victory either! Believe it, and you will! Faith is victory! Jesus Christ has already won the victory over every foe: the world, the flesh, and the devil (Hebrews 2:14; Colossians 2:14, 15; 1 John 3:8, 4:4). You don't have any victories to win. Jesus won them all two thousand years ago. Once you believe it, stand on it and claim it. His victories are your victories!

Notice that it is this kind of "God has" faith that provides salvation. You must believe God has already provided salvation in and through Jesus Christ. The lost sinner must come to God and accept God's provision by repenting of sin and saying, "Thank You, Jesus, it is already done." Notice also, the way you received salvation is the same way you receive daily victory and guidance. If you have faith, you have the substance. Whatever your need is, just believe it is already yours, and it is yours.

May God add to your asking-believing. "Lord, teach us to pray in faith, claiming what is already ours in Christ."

Resources

    1. See Luke 11:9–13.

    2. Chapter 4, "Can a Christian Lose His Salvation?" discusses the problem of guilt and forgiveness in detail.

Chapter 5

*Praying in the name of Jesus
is a believer's carte blanche to
God the Father. Our faith in that
holy name is our access to the
throne room.*

5

Why Do We Pray in Jesus' Name?

When I was a small boy, my parents began to expose me to religion by enrolling me in a Roman Catholic school. My first three years of schooling came from this parochial education. The first prayer I ever remember praying audibly was a memorized "grace" at the lunch table in this school. Countless numbers of Catholic children have recited this little prayer to God before eating: "Bless us, O Lord, in these Thy gifts, which we are about to receive from Thy bounty, through Jesus Christ our Lord, Amen."

That was my first prayer, and not a bad one at that. However, that last phrase used to intrigue me—". . . through Jesus Christ our Lord." As I grew older, I began to hear others "sign off" their petitions with ". . . in Jesus' name, Amen." My curious mind pondered the "why" of this practice of praying "in Jesus' name." I was an adult before the real truth of this common verbal exercise was driven home to my heart.

A Simple Request

Jesus was giving His disciples profound teaching on obedience, the Holy Spirit, and prayer in John 14–16. In the midst of that teaching, three times our Lord told His followers to ask things of God "in My name": "Truly, truly, I say to you, if you shall ask the Father for anything, He will give it to you *in My name.* Until now you have asked for nothing in My name; ask, and you will receive, that your joy may be made full" (John 16:23, 24, emphasis mine). Christ had already urged this in chapter 14 and again in chapter 15 (*see* John 14:13, 14 and John 15:16). This repetition was no doubt used to drive home this simple yet profound principle: the way to God's heart is through His Son's name.

Nothing Asked, Nothing Received. We must remember that this teaching was unique and new to these Jewish followers. Never before in history had a Jew prayed to Jehovah God in the name of a man! That's why Jesus says, "Until now you have asked for nothing in My name" (John 16:23). This is revolutionary teaching. It lies at the very center of Christian theology. Jesus says there is a new path to God's throne that has never been traveled. There is a new phone number to God's private line that has never been used—dial it! "Until now, you've never come to the Father in My name. Now do it, and My Father will give you whatever you ask," says the Lord Jesus.

What a paradox! Until that time, no one had ever prayed to God "in Jesus' name." Probably this was not done by the early followers of Christ until after Pentecost. It took the prompting of the indwelling Holy Spirit to get the early church to pray in Jesus' name.

Today, millions pray daily prayers, often by rote and then casually close their prayers with a meaningless "in Jesus' name." Once the church understands the power and potency of the name of Jesus, our prayers will bring Pentecost again. It was faith in the power of that Name that ignited the early church, and it can ignite faith and fire in your heart when and if you understand why God honors the name of Jesus.

In My Name

Why pray in Jesus' name? Why not Buddha, or Allah, or some other great religious teacher or prophet? To pray in Jesus' name is to acknowledge that our access to God's presence is through the atoning work of Jesus Christ. Just as the Jews could not enter the Holy Place in the temple without blood atonement (on Yom Kippur), even so the sinner cannot enter the presence of Holy God without the shed blood of Jesus Christ. Only through His death, burial, resurrection, and ascension can we have a Father-Child relationship with God. A sinner without a savior has no hope of forgiveness. "Without shedding of blood there is no forgiveness. . . . For Christ did not enter a holy place made with hands, a mere copy of the true one, but into heaven itself, now to appear in the presence of God for us" (Hebrews 9:22, 24); ". . . therefore, brethren, we have confidence to enter the holy place by the blood of Jesus" (Hebrews 10:19).

That's why we come to God's throne in Jesus' name. It is asking on the merits of His righteousness. It is like saying to God, "God, I ask these things, not because of who I am or because of my goodness. I ask because Jesus told me to come to You and to tell You He sent me. He said You'd answer my prayer for His sake, not mine."

When Father Owns the Store. Let me illustrate this principle. Suppose you need groceries. You go to the supermarket and buy everything you ever needed in the way of food and household commodities. You come to the checkout stand with ten cartloads of food and other merchandise. The checker rings up the total on the register. The register tape reaches to the floor; it's an enormous amount of money. The checker looks at you in wonderment and with a bit of suspicion. Let's say the total comes to $5,000. Now you say to the checker, "Let me have that tape; I'm just going to sign it." The checker is astonished. "Sign it? Who do you think you are, the owner?" You reply,

"No, as a matter of fact, I am not the owner, but my father is. I am the owner's only son, heir to the fortune."

This is what Jesus means when He tells us to ask the Father in His name. Everything that belongs to God the Father also belongs to His only begotten Son. Jesus is co-owner of the store. He has told His Father that we can sign the ticket in His name. Father is honor-bound to answer your prayer in Jesus' name just as though *Christ Himself* were doing the asking. The believer is so united to Christ that our asking is His asking through His Spirit in us. Incredible truth!

Using the Rod of God

Earlier, we discussed Exodus 17 and Moses' "Rod of God." We concluded that our rod is faith in the name of Jesus. In Mark 16:17, Jesus tells us to make use of His name, even to putting demons to flight. It is exciting to me to watch those early disciples begin to practice what Jesus preached. After Pentecost, Peter and John are on the way to the temple to pray. Jesus is gone back to the Father, but His Spirit now indwells these two men. Outside the temple, Peter and John meet a crippled man, begging from those on their way to temple prayers. The beggar man asks for money. Peter stops and a thought crosses his mind—a thought no doubt prompted by the Spirit of Jesus within him: "Peter, use your rod. Try it out. Make use of My name, ask the Father. Use My name and see the miracle." Impulsively, Peter says to the cripple, "I do not possess silver and gold, but what I do have I give to you: In the name of Jesus Christ the Nazarene—walk!" (*See* Acts 3:1–6.) There, for the first time, one of the twelve did it. They took Jesus at His word, made use of His name, and moved into the miraculous. Later, when the Jewish authorities questioned Peter and John as to how the man was healed, they joyously replied, "on the basis of faith in His name, it is the name of Jesus which has strengthened this man ..." (Acts 3:16).

Let us always remember that the name of Jesus is the Christian's cosmic credit card, always honored in the courts of heaven. Put your faith behind it, and God will put His power in it.

Lord, teach us to pray in Jesus' name.

Chapter 6

*Satan has the power to hold the answer
back—for a while; to delay the result—for a time.
He has not the power to hold it back finally, if
someone understands and prays with quiet, steady
persistence. The real pitch of prayer therefore
is Satanward.*

S. D. Gordon,
Quiet Talks on Prayer

6

What Is Spiritual Warfare?

The Christian life is a life of warfare. The Christian is a part of an eternal struggle between good and evil. To be a child of God is to fight against the forces of evil all the days of your life. Yet, so very few are truly aware of this spiritual conflict. The vast majority of church members act as though the enemy is dead and they are at last in Zion. Someone has said that the old ship of Zion is not a luxury liner on which we sail leisurely into heaven's harbor; it is a battleship, a man of war in which we engage the enemy daily.

What then is this spiritual warfare? Who is the enemy? What are our weapons? How is this war ever fought? These are the questions for which we shall seek God's answers from His Word.

The Enemy

Paul, writing to the Ephesian believers, describes spiritual warfare and the nature of the enemy: "Finally, be strong in the Lord, and in the strength of His might. Put on the full armor of God, that you may be able to stand firm against the schemes of the devil. For our struggle is not against flesh and blood, but against the rulers, against the powers, against the world forces of this darkness, against the spiritual forces of wickedness in the heavenly places" (Ephesians 6:10–12).

Our enemy Satan is a mighty foe, a fallen archangel whose heart is full of hatred toward the Lord Jesus and His kingdom. Satan is the spirit ruler of a kingdom of darkness. He leads "world forces of spiritual wickedness." Whether or not you believe in a personal Satan and demon forces is vital to your victory or defeat in this conflict. To pretend there is no enemy is to guarantee your defeat. Folks who do not believe the devil exists are those who have more devil in them than anyone else!

A "Spirit" War.   Notice Scripture describes this warfare as "spiritual" in nature. We are not fighting in the physical realm—"For our struggle is not against flesh and blood." This is an invisible war fought against invisible foes—Satan and his minions. Many believers are losing this war by default because they simply have not shown up for the war. Satan wins unopposed, because the Christian refuses to fight in this "spiritual" battle. Mark it down: *this war is spiritual, not physical.* Church buildings and budgets will not win this struggle. Church committees and charities will not defeat "spiritual wickedness in high places."

The point we must understand is that our daily problems are not physical in nature. They only seem to be. Behind every physical problem, there is a deeper, truer, spiritual problem or reality. The physical is only the tool of the spiritual. Matthew 16:21–23 illustrates this truth for us. Jesus has just foretold His coming death in Jerusalem. Simon Peter speaks up, saying, "God forbid it, Lord! This shall never happen to You" (verse 22). Now, notice the rebuke Jesus gives, "Get behind Me, Satan!..." Our Lord does not rebuke Peter but rather the spirit power behind Peter's words. Satan had spoken through Peter's mind and voice. The problem was not Peter, but the power behind Peter: Satan. You see, often the problem is not in the physical at all, but rather spirit forces at work behind the scenes manipulating the physical realm.

Again, we are daily fighting a spiritual, unseen war. In Ephesians, Paul describes our "struggle." The King James Version translates this word as "wrestle." The idea of this word is hand-to-hand combat. This war is your own personal battle. To be saved is to be involved in struggle against these world forces of darkness. Christian, you are involved whether you like it or not. Sadly, so few Christians are even aware of this conflict. Satan is very determined to defeat each Christian, and naturally he prefers to do so without the believer even being aware of his presence.

Spiritual Weapons. If we are to fight a spirit warfare, we shall need spiritual weapons. Our armor and weaponry must be adaptable to the enemy and his tactics. Paul describes the Christian's armor when he says, "Therefore, take up the full armor of God, that you may be able to resist in the evil day, and having done everything, to stand firm. Stand firm therefore, having girded your loins with truth, and having put on the breastplate of righteousness, and having shod your feet with the preparation of the gospel of peace; in addition to all, taking up the shield of faith with which you will be able to extinguish all the flaming missiles of the evil one. And take the helmet of salvation, and the sword of the Spirit, which is the Word of God" (Ephesians 6:13–17).

Here is a picture of you and me dressed in battle fatigues, armed and ready for battle. The belt of truth, breastplate of righteousness, marching boots, a shield of faith, helmet of salvation, and the sword of the Spirit; these are your weapons. What armor! You are equipped for hand-to-hand combat with the devil himself. You are ready: show me the battle, take me to the front lines. Let's get it on! Okay, here is the war; listen to Paul's words in the next verse: "With all prayer and petition pray at all times in the Spirit, and with this view, be on the alert with all perseverance and petition for all the saints" (Ephesians 6:18).

Prayer Is the War

Now, can you beat that? You are dressed in battle gear, ready to fight, and Paul tells you to pray! Pray? That's right, pray. You see, disappointing as it may seem, prayer *is* the war. The armor is merely preparation for prayer. The Christian warrior is a prayer warrior. This spiritual warfare is fought by an army marching on its knees. Our enemy is spiritual, so we must use our greatest spiritual weapons against him. Prayer is the means whereby we enter the spirit conflict. Here is where many churches and Christian leaders are missing out on the war. We have thought that our problems were lack of funds, facilities, or organizations. If only our church had this or that, then we could do great things for God. God help us! We are never going to defeat the devil with buildings, budgets, or bombs. If and when we overcome the Evil One, it will be through the power of prayer. This has always been God's way.

The Evangelist and Revival. I am an evangelist. Over the last twenty-three years, I have preached in hundreds of churches in America and around the world. Seldom has a church truly believed that prayer is the battle. To prepare for a week of preaching, the average pastor will put ads in the paper, on TV, and posters in business places, announcing the coming crusade. He will promote attendance with gimmicks and gadgets to get people to the crusade. All of this is good and proper, but this is the physical, when the battle is spiritual. Seldom does the church put on the armor and go to war in prayer. I mean real intercessory prayer. You know, get down in the trenches and "wrestle" in hand-to-hand combat until the victory is won. It's much easier just to promote and to go hear the evangelist preach. Then we wonder why there is no great moving of God's Spirit among the people.

Two weeks ago (at this writing), I was in Romania preaching. There, in a communist country, we preached to crowds of three to four thousand every night in a building that seats only eight hundred. There was no advertising in the paper, no television, and no posters. There was no promotion, because it is illegal in the communist system to promote religion. What a blessing! I almost wish it were illegal in the West. Then maybe we couldn't depend on the flesh and we would be forced to depend upon the Lord. In Romania, the believers face the Prince of Darkness every day. They are in a struggle for survival. Prayer is their one resource, and they are using it as a mighty weapon to tear down satanic strongholds. Thousands are coming to Christ in the midst of great opposition and persecution. Prayer is the war. When we don't pray, we lose by default.

Prayer and Evangelism.   Evangelism is a spiritual warfare won by intercession. Whenever a lost person is born again into God's kingdom, you can count on it: someone prayed for that person. Someone "stood in the gap" for that lost soul. Only when we drive the enemy off the battlefield of the human heart is the lost man free to respond to God's grace. This is why I repeat that preaching, witnessing, programs, and all other church work are good and necessary, but it is not the real conflict. Satan fears us most when we take our spiritual weapons and use them against him in prayer.

Earlier, we cited the example of Moses and Joshua fighting against Amalek. The battle is recorded in Exodus 17:9–16. Remember, as Joshua was fighting the battle down on the plains, Moses was praying for him up on the mountain. Moses was fighting the real battle against the spiritual forces of evil that were empowering the idolatrous King Amalek. Moses intercedes and Joshua prevails against Amalek. You see, Joshua might as well have been a third-string quarterback called in at the last quarter when the Israelites were ahead 100 to 0. As long as Moses was doing battle, it was easy for him to move in and "discomfit" Amalek (Exodus 17:13 KJV).

Satan Opposes Our Prayers.   When a spirit-filled, believing child of God begins to pray excitedly, Satan trembles. He knows that such praying is supernatural. It puts God in the fight. He cannot win against such weapons. This is why Satan will actively oppose your prayer life. Have you observed how difficult it is to spend time in prayer? We find time for every other "religious" activity; we attend church, Bible class, and even witness now and then. However, when it comes to prayer—real communion with God—it seems every conflict imaginable will occur. This is Satan's work. He will hinder your prayer life whenever possible. Prayer is warfare, make no mistake about it!

Dr. Stephen Alford was for many years pastor of the Calvary Baptist Church in New York City. I once heard the great man describe how Satan would oppose his prayer life. He said that for many years he could not understand why his thoughts would ramble in prayer. Often vile, hateful or lustful thoughts would enter his prayer time. Finally, he discovered the warfare. He came to realize that these thoughts were "fiery darts" shot from Satan's bow to destroy his intercessions and prayers.

Praying is more than meeting God. It is also the time we engage the enemy. This is not to imply that in praying we address the devil. God forbid! However, he is there to oppose us, and we must deal with him. In a later chapter, we will discuss this matter of dealing with the devil through the "binding and loosing" mentioned in Matthew 18:18. For now, it is enough to know that Satan does oppose our prayers. He can even delay the answers to prayer.

Daniel 10.　The clearest illustration that prayer is a spiritual warfare is found in the Old Testament. Daniel 10:13 describes young Daniel the Prophet spending three weeks in fasting and prayer. After this period of intense spiritual conflict, an angel arrives, sent to Daniel in answer to his prayer. Now, God has never sent an angel (that I could see) to answer one of my prayers, but then I've never prayed and fasted as earnestly as Daniel did! When the angel speaks to Daniel, he says a most remarkable thing, "Do not be afraid, Daniel, for from the first day that you set your heart on understanding this and on humbling yourself before your God, your words were heard, and I have come in response to your words" (Daniel 10:12). Notice the phrase, "from the first day." The angel started to come to Daniel from the first day he prayed. Why did it take him three weeks to get there? In the next verse, the angel explains his delay: "But the prince of the kingdom of Persia was withstanding me for twenty-one days; then behold, Michael, one of the chief princes, came to help me. . . ."

This is mind-boggling! Here Daniel is praying, and in the unseen, invisible world of the spirit, a battle begins. God sends an angel (messenger) to answer Daniel, but the angel is opposed by the prince of Persia (an ancient allusion to Satan). For twenty-one days the angel battles Satan himself, all because Daniel is praying and fasting! The angel is no match for Satan, so God finally sends Michael the archangel to end the conflict, and victory is won. Satan was preventing the answer to Daniel's prayer. What do you think about that? That's a mind stretcher, isn't it? Well, whether you take this passage to be symbolic or literal, one fact is clear: Praying puts us into the realm of the spirit where the real fight exists. Prayer is warfare, and it is so vital to God that it can even put angels to work. That's right; your prayers, lifted up in faith and sincerity, can activate the hosts of heaven. Scripture tells us that God's angels are ministering spirits sent out to render service for those who touch the supernatural with their prayers (*see* Hebrews 1:13, 14).

A Call to Arms. At this point, we've come to see that genuine praying is at the very heart of the church's ministry. Praying is so much more than saying thanks to God, or asking Him for things. Prayer is a call to arms. It is very serious business. Through prayer, we touch heaven and attack hell. It is not for the faint of heart or weak in faith. Most of the remainder of this book will be devoted to the "deeper things" of intercession and warfare. You may think we're already so deep we are in over our heads! Again we join with Paul in his prayer "that the eyes of your heart may be enlightened." Lord, teach us to pray.

Chapter 7

*There is a serious deficiency in the
outworking of the spirit-filled life if it
does not issue in a revitalizing experience
in the realm of prayer.*

Arthur Wallis
Pray in the Spirit

7

Becoming a Prayer Warrior

*What Preparations Are Necessary
to Pray Effectively?*

Every Christian has the right to pray and the ability to pray. However, not every Christian is prepared to enter into spiritual warfare. The deeper things of intercession and prayer are reserved for those who are equipped. Like a young soldier going to boot camp for basic training, the Christian must "put on the full armor of God" before he can be "strong in the Lord and in the strength of His might" (Ephesians 6:11, 10).

The Boot Camp of Prayer

The armor Paul speaks of in Ephesians 6:10–17 is really preparation for prayer. Because prayer is where we meet God and also encounter the enemy Satan, we must be prepared by putting on God's full armor. The apostle Paul gives us sound advice on preparing for a ministry of prayer. He tells us to do three things:

We are to pray by "standing firm."
We are to pray by using the "sword of the Spirit."
We are to pray by praying "in the Spirit."

75

Pray Standing Firm. We are encouraged to stand fast against "the schemes of the devil" (Ephesians 6:11) by putting on the full armor of God. What Paul means is that our foundation for prayer must be the completed work of Christ. We stand on the victory He won at the cross. Also, we are to live a holy and obedient life before God. We are armored with the breastplate of righteousness; we have marching shoes on to show our obedience, to go where He commands. So we pray from a position of strength. We can pray with boldness. There will be more about our victory over the enemy in the next chapter when we discuss the weapons of our warfare.

Pray With the Sword. "And take ... the sword of the Spirit, which is the word of God" (Ephesians 6:17). An effective prayer warrior uses his weapon of the Word of God. The sword of the Word is an offensive weapon in the life of a praying Christian. Those who pray effectively have learned to use the Bible in their prayer life. In fact, power in prayer and knowledge of the Bible are inseparable. Do you know how to use the Word in your prayer life? Let me suggest some ways:

- *Hold the Word of God up to the Lord.*
  Use the Word when you talk to God. Remember, the Bible is a book of promises the Father has made to His children. We can expect God to keep His Word. Hold Him to it in faith. Quote it back to Him in prayer. Often, when I'm praying, Scripture will be a large portion of the context of my praying. At times I'll begin my time with God just by reading it to Him, I especially like to read the Psalms out loud in my praying. The value of holding the Word up to the throne is that the biblical promises are like an "IOU" from God to us. We are coheirs with Christ, so everything that belongs to Christ is our inheritance also. Praying with the sword is claiming your new birthrights. The believer comes to the throne of God and says, "Father, I am Your child,

and You said that You would supply all my needs [Philippians 4:19], and I am going to hold You to Your Word today."

- *Hold the Word of God up against the devil.*
Also, when you pray, learn to use the sword of the Spirit against the enemy. Satan hates and fears the truth of God's Word. Use it on him—it cuts him to shreds! The sword of the Word can drive Satan off the battlefield altogether; he must retreat. There will be times in prayer that Satan will attack you with evil thoughts, desires, or destructions. He will do all in his power to hinder your prayer time. Hold the Word up to him. Isaiah 54:17 says, "No weapon that is formed against you shall prosper. . . ." The devil knows he is a defeated foe, but he runs a bluff much of the time. You must let him know *you* know he's defeated. Quote the Word to him. Often I just rebuke him to his face: "Satan, you are a liar." The Bible says, ". . . the Son of God appeared for this purpose, that He might destroy the works of the devil" (1 John 3:8). Satan cannot withstand the truth of God's Word; he will flee.

- *Hold up the Word to lift the soul.*
At times, you may not feel like praying. Quote the Word out loud for yourself and God. Often the Holy Spirit will use the Scriptures to lift your soul upward, to prepare your heart for prayer and intercession.

- *Pray in the Spirit.*
Paul then tells us to enter this spiritual warfare by "praying at all times in the Spirit." You and I cannot become prayer warriors without these three preparations. We learn to pray standing firm on the completed work of Christ, praying with the Word of God as our offensive weapon, and praying in the power and infilling of the Holy Spirit. As previously discussed, real

praying is Holy Spirit infused. It is praying that is God breathed and sustained. Only as we are yielded to the Spirit of Holy God can we hope to become holy warriors in prayer. We've mentioned the sword of God's Word as a weapon in prayer, but now I want to turn our attention to two other mighty weapons of prayer warfare: the cross and our identification with Christ.

Chapter 8

From strength to strength go on;
Wrestle, and fight, and pray;
Tread all the powers of darkness down,
And win the well-fought day.

Charles Wesley

8

Using the Weapons of Spiritual Warfare

What Are the Weapons of Our Warfare?

Praying takes many forms. Prayer can be pure worship, just communicating praise to God. Prayer can be pure work; at times, the hardest work you'll ever do will be done in intercession for others. Then, of course, prayer can be warfare. When praying is of the Spirit, from the heart, it will engage the enemy. Because there are times when prayer is spiritual warfare, we'll need spiritual weapons to defeat the "spiritual wickedness in high places" we will encounter.

A Battle Plan

Every Christian needs a basic understanding of how spiritual warfare is fought and the weapons needed to overpower the enemy. The disciples of Jesus once came against a demon-possessed boy and could not cast out the demon. The father of the boy brought the lad to Jesus, who immediately cast out the evil spirit. Later, the disciples asked our Lord why they had not been able to cast out the demon. Jesus replied:

> Because of the littleness of your faith; for truly I say to you, if you have faith as a mustard seed, you shall say to

this mountain, "Move from here to there," and it shall move; and nothing shall be impossible to you. [Then, some manuscripts add the following words:] But this kind does not go out except by prayer and fasting.

Matthew 17:20, 21

We are much like those early disciples. We become powerless against the demonic forces we face every day. We have the resources to move these mountains if only we had the faith and understanding to apply them.

In this chapter, we shall study the weapons God has given us to live victoriously and to pray powerfully.

The Weapon of the Cross

In Ephesians 6:11–14, Paul tells us repeatedly to "stand firm." In other words, Paul says "hold your ground." The "ground" he was referring to was the ground Jesus Christ won for us when He died and rose again. Calvary was a spiritual battlefield in which Jesus conquered enemy territory for God and a lost world. In His victory, He conquered the world, the flesh, and the devil.

In Colossians 2:13–15, we have two beautiful "word" pictures describing our Lord's victory won at the cross and empty tomb. Paul says,

And when you were dead in your transgressions and the uncircumcision of your flesh, He made you alive together with Him, having forgiven us all our transgressions, having cancelled out the certificate of debt consisting of decrees against us and which was hostile to us; and He has taken it out of the way, having nailed it to the cross. When He had disarmed the rulers and authorities, He made a public display of them, having triumphed over them through Him.

The "certificate of debt" that Paul refers to is an allusion to the Roman law of Paul's day. When Jesus Christ was crucified, the soldiers nailed an inscription above His head on the cross. It read, "King of the Jews." Have you ever wondered why this was done? This inscription was a certificate of debt, a legal charge brought against Jesus by His accusers. In Roman times, it was common for a legal charge to be brought before a judge. The judge would then rule guilty or innocent. If guilty, the accusation or certificate of debt[1] would be attached to the cell door of the imprisoned, or in our Lord's case, nailed to the cross. Therefore, all could see and know the legal charge for which the guilty was accused. Jesus was accused of treason against Rome as King of the Jews; hence the inscription over His head.

Now, Paul says in Colossians 2:14 that when Jesus died He blotted out the "certificate of debt . . . which was hostile to us." Notice, this legal charge or certificate was "against us," not against Christ. Thus, there was another certificate of debt on that cross; it was invisible, but there nonetheless. It was a debt we owed that Jesus paid by His death. You see, Satan is the accuser. He has a sin list on every sinner. He brings his accusation against the sinner at the throne of God. Satan presents his certificate of debt before God. We sinners are guilty as charged, and "the wages of sin is death" (Romans 6:23). Now, what did God do for us? He took the certificate of debt, nailed it to the cross, and blotted it out with the precious blood of His only Son. God settled our case out of court, on the cross.

Satan's Only Weapon. The truth of this for us to apply is that Satan's only weapon to use against us is our sins. Jesus has blotted out, totally removed, our sins. Satan has no legal claim on us. Jesus died for the sins of the whole world (1 John 2:2). Therefore, by His death on the cross, Jesus has defeated the devil. That's the first word picture Paul uses in Colossians 2.

Colossians 2:15. The second word picture is from Roman military conquest. Jesus made an "open disgrace" of the devil through His cross. This "open disgrace" is a reference to Cae-

sar's conquest in battle. When the Romans would defeat an
army, they would disgrace the enemy by disrobing the defeated king or general and make him and his conquered army
march behind Caesar's chariot (or the Roman commander) in
chains and stripped of armor and weapons. When the Romans
would march back into Rome, the people would mock the defeated slaves in chains behind the victorious Caesar. Now,
when did Jesus disgrace the devil? At the cross He defeated
him, but when did He openly disgrace him? When He rose
again from the grave! When Jesus conquered death, He "disarmed the rulers and authorities, He made a public display of
them" (Colossians 2:15). Satan is a defeated and disgraced foe.
He has no weapons to use against the blood-bought child of
God.

Using the Cross as a Weapon.   How does this relate to spiritual
warfare? In every way this war is fixed. We have already won.
The victory need only be appropriated through prayer. Satan
has no claim on us or on those for whom we pray. When we
pray using our faith in this completed work of Christ, we bring
Calvary's victory "up to date" in our current situation. Often,
in praying for lost people, I will remind the devil that Jesus has
already redeemed my lost friend. I command Satan to release
his hold on that person for whom Christ died. I will "plead the
blood" of Christ against him. Revelation 12:11 says, "they
overcame him [Satan] by the blood of the Lamb, and because
of the word of their testimony." We can overcome him the
same way. The words of Martin Luther's great hymn come to
mind: ". . . we tremble not for him; / . . . one little word shall
fell him."[2]

His Victory, Our Victory

Again, I want to stress this principle of our total identification with Christ. His victory was for us; we share in it. We are
"in Him" and He is in us. Therefore, that which is historically
true can be made experientially true in our daily lives. Living

victoriously as a Christian is not that complicated. It is simply resting in the victory of the cross. It is, by faith, bringing Calvary up to date in our lives.

Not long ago, I wrote to a pastor friend of mine who was to go on trial in Romania. The charges against him were false and unjustified. He faced a two-year prison sentence. When I returned home from Romania, I notified many friends to pray for his upcoming trial and release. We sent letters and telegrams to let the authorities know this pastor had friends in the West. Our ultimate weapon was prayer. I personally gave him to God for protection. I also rebuked Satan and commanded him to "cease and desist" harassing this dear Romanian brother. I brought the cross of Jesus into the fight. Shortly thereafter, word came to us that the charges had been dropped and the trial dismissed. Praise the Lord!

We must not let Satan bluff us, blackmail us, or in any other way deceive us. We are the victors, not the victims. We in Christ are winners, always and at all times. Believe it, act like it, and pray accordingly.

For though we walk in the flesh, we do not war according to the flesh, for the weapons of our warfare are not of the flesh, but divinely powerful for the destruction of fortresses. We are destroying speculations and every lofty thing raised up against the knowledge of God, and we are taking every thought captive to the obedience of Christ.

2 Corinthians 10:3-5

Prayer Weapons. These verses tell us what our prayer weapons are to be used for. They are "mighty through God to the pulling down of strong holds" (v. 4 KJV). What are these strongholds we are to destroy with our prayer weapons? This phrase probably has reference to areas of bondage (sin habits) in people's lives. Many folks have satanic strongholds of guilt, doubt, fear, rebellion, and overt sin. These are the result of years of habitual sin. These areas of bondage hold people captive to do Satan's will. Through intercessory prayer, we can set captives free.

Suppose you have a friend who is in bondage to a sin habit such as drugs or alcohol. As a prayer warrior, your task is to go to battle for your friend. In prayer, we can pull down those strongholds by forbidding Satan to harass, impress, or tempt that person. We can command him in Jesus' name to loose his grip on that person's will, his mind, or his body. What a fantastic ministry *real* praying can be.

Applying to Victory for Daily Needs.   In prayer, we use all our weapons. First, through our position in Christ, we can come to God boldly claiming His promises. Then, we have the weapons of the blood, the cross, the Word, and the mighty name of Jesus to enter the conflict in intercession for others. These weapons are mighty in the hands of a Spirit-filled believer who walks in faith and obedience. In the following chapter, we will study further the authority of the believer as he uses his prayer weapons.

Resources

1. The King James Version translates the phrase as "handwriting of ordinance."

2. "A Mighty Fortress Is Our God," by Martin Luther.

Chapter 9

"Truly I say to you, whatever you shall bind on earth shall have been bound in heaven; and whatever you loose on earth shall have been loosed in heaven. Again I say to you, that if two of you agree on earth about anything that they may ask, it shall be done for them by My Father who is in heaven. For where two or three have gathered together in My name, there I am in their midst."

Matthew 18:18–20

9

What Are the Keys of the Kingdom?

Learning to Use the Spiritual Keys That
Unlock Heaven's Doors

Recently, I was leading a Bible conference for a group of college students, when one bright young lady asked me a very challenging question. She asked, "What did Jesus mean by this statement in Matthew 16:19 when He told Simon Peter, 'I will give you the keys of the kingdom of heaven; and whatever you shall bind on earth shall have been bound in heaven, and whatever you shall loose on earth shall have been loosed in heaven'?" Her question was really a two-pronged question. What are the "keys" to the kingdom of heaven, and second, what is meant by the "binding and loosing" in this statement? These are good questions, and a simple answer is not possible because there are some complicating factors.

Two Texts

Notice I have quoted two texts here—one in the chapter epigraph, the other in the student's question—both of which repeat the idea of binding and loosing. Jesus stated this principle on two different occasions, both remembered and recorded by Matthew. Matthew 18:18 records this statement in the context of church discipline and prayer, while Matthew 16:19 records it as addressed to Simon Peter and the other disciples at Caesarea Phillipi in extreme northern Galilee.

What Jesus meant by this teaching is very important to us today. It has enormous value to us in prayer, especially prayer for other people, yet very few believers today have any idea what these words mean.

Roman Catholic Teaching. My early church training was Roman Catholic. The verses of Matthew 16:18 and 19 are an important part of Roman theology. Catholic theologians take verse eighteen to refer to Peter as the rock foundation upon which Christ built the church. They say these words of Jesus mean that Christ gave to Peter the keys to the kingdom of heaven. These keys are the power to forgive sin; therefore, Peter and his papal successors have the power to tell heaven whom to forgive and whom not to forgive.

As evidence of this fact, you can visit the Vatican in Rome, and in St. Peter's Cathedral there is a life-size marble statue of Peter kneeling before Christ. There chiseled in stone beside the kneeling statue is this verse: "I will give unto Thee [meaning Peter] the keys of the kingdom of heaven; and whatsoever Thou shalt loose on earth shall be loosed in heaven." Thus, Roman theology uses this verse to teach the ascending of Peter and his power to forgive sin.

Solving a Difficult Problem. Obviously, this is not the interpretation of these verses that I find accurate. I have no quarrel with the Roman Catholic church except to say that such an interpretation of the words of Jesus is misleading. It doesn't take a serious Bible student to discover this fact. In fact, there is a threefold error involved.

First of all, to whom were these words addressed? To Peter alone, or to the church in general? Those who say Jesus gave the keys to Peter face a difficult textual problem. This is true for two reasons. First, Peter is not the "rock" foundation upon which Jesus built His church. Jesus Himself is the foundation of His church. The word for Peter in Greek is *Petros,* which means "a stone or little rock." The word translated "rock" in the same verse (Matthew 16:18) is another Greek word, *petra,* which means "bedrock," massive rock, or foundation rock. Peter is only a *petros,* a piece of the *petra,* not the *petra* itself. The Greek language used here is very specific and distinctive. Most modern scholars agree that the "rock" foundation upon which Christ has been building His church is the divine revelation revealed to Simon in verse sixteen, that Jesus is indeed the Christ. This divine revelation comes to every true believer. When the Holy Spirit reveals Christ to the human heart, that individual must do as Simon did—confess what the Spirit revealed. That is how people are born again into the true church. That is how we each become a "piece" of the rock. Each believer is a *petros,* part of the *petra.*

Peter or the Church.   The second reason for rejecting the idea that Jesus gave to Peter (and thus his papal successors) supernatural power to forgive sins is much less complicated. The Lord Jesus repeats this statement about the power to bind and loose in Matthew 18. Here, the context is remarkably different. Here Peter is not addressed at all. These words are used in connection with prayer. In fact, Jesus says that "if two of you agree on earth about anything that they may ask, it shall be done for them by My Father who is in heaven" (Matthew 18:19). Notice, "if any two of you agree," you can ask and receive. How general can He make it—"any two of you"? Thus, any two of you can bind and loose here on earth.

These words are spoken by Christ to the church in general. In fact, the preceding verses deal with the church disciplining its members. Jesus tells us how to reprove a brother "caught" in a sin. His conclusion to that statement reveals our greatest weapon: if just two Christians can agree on God's will, they, through prayer, can "bind and loose." This is extremely important. Matthew 18 teaches us that this power to "bind and loose" is a prayer weapon to be used by the church. It is *not* a special power given to a select group of clergy who are in some way mystical descendents of Simon Peter.

What Is This Binding and Loosing? The third error has to do with the meaning of Jesus' words, "You shall bind on earth" and "You shall loose on earth." Did Jesus mean to imply that Peter or anyone else could actually forgive sins? I think not. Neither pope nor priest has that divine prerogative; only God Himself can forgive sins. This can be easily demonstrated; a careful look at the text in Matthew 16:19 and Matthew 18:18 will reveal this fact. The King James Version of the New Testament, known as the "authorized" version for 350 years, translates these verses this way: ". . . and whatsoever ye shall bind on earth shall be bound in heaven: and whatsoever ye shall loose on earth shall be loosed in heaven." These verbs are translated as though they are a simple future tense. If this were correct, the translation would also be correct. The meaning then would be that "heaven" is waiting for "earth" to tell it what to do. Heaven takes its cue from earth. Thus, anything that I here on earth forbid (bind) or permit (loose), then God must obey by binding or loosing. This is the position taken by those who teach that man can forgive sins. This error has occurred by a failure to translate correctly the tenses of the verbs used. The verbs are not future tense, but rather, they are a complicated future passive periphrastic perfect indicative.[1] In fact, in both verses, the first verb is aorist (past tense) and the second is the perfect passive. Neither is in the future tense. The *Interlinear Greek-English New Testament*[2] translates the Greek perfect as "shall having been bound" (or loosed). The New American Standard Bible correctly brings out the sense of the perfect periphrastic construction by translating the verbs "whatever you shall bind on earth shall have been bound in heaven; and whatever you loose on earth shall have been loosed in heaven." Notice the "shall have been" emphasis. This is the correct rendering of the text. Just what difference does this make? It means that what Jesus really said is just the opposite of how the King James Version reads. Heaven does not take its cue from earth! Never! Earth takes its cue from heaven. We can only bind and loose what has already been bound and loosed. Whatever Jesus has already forbidden or permitted, we can claim in prayer. This binding and loosing is our authority in Christ, not to forgive sins, but rather to take authority over the enemy in intercession. Binding and loosing is a prayer weapon.

Hog-tie the Devil

Have you ever wished you could hog-tie the devil for just one day? Wouldn't it be great just to command him to leave you or your loved ones alone? Friend, lying at the very heart of Jesus' teaching on binding and loosing is this principle—our power over the evil one. Because the Lord Jesus has already rendered the devil powerless (Hebrews 2:14), we share in that victory. We look up to heaven, seeing our Lord's complete victory; then we, by faith, use our "keys" to command Satan to loose our lost friends, or command him to be bound from oppressing them. Every day in prayer we can forbid and permit, binding and loosing. These "keys" are our mighty weapons to the pulling down of strongholds spoken of in 2 Corinthians 10:4.

Setting Captives Free. This marvelous principle lies at the very heart of intercessory prayer. In a previous book, we discussed how to pray for lost people.[3] In that chapter it is emphasized that a lost sinner is held captive by the devil. He is in spiritual chains. He is blinded by the evil one so that he cannot see the truth of the gospel. Satan has both blinded and bound the lost person. He needs emancipation and illumination. It is the task of a believing church to pray him free. That's right, pray him free. Once we have driven the enemy off the battlefield of the human will, then that unsaved person is once again free to make a moral choice regarding Jesus Christ. When you meet a godless sinner, you and I should pity that person. He is in the "snare" of the evil one (*see* 2 Timothy 2:26). Without our warfare in his behalf, the sinner is hopelessly lost, yet with our persistent intercession, Satan will loose him and he can choose freely to come to Christ. I do not mean to imply that every person we pray for will be saved, but I do believe many would be saved if the church could only believe and take authority over the enemy. Jesus has given us the keys to the kingdom of heaven—let's learn to use them! The gates of hell cannot stand against a praying church.

Resources

1. A. T. Robertson, *Word Studies in the New Testament,* vol. 1 (Nashville, Tennessee: Broadman Press, 1930), p. 149.

2. *The International Greek-English New Testament* (London: Samuel Bagster and Sons, 1964).

3. *See* chapter 16 in *Questions Non-Christians Ask* (Old Tappan, New Jersey: Fleming H. Revell Company, 1977), pp. 145–153.

Chapter 10

Much time spent with God is the secret of all successful praying. Prayer which is felt as a mighty force is the mediate or immediate product of much time spent with God. Our short prayers owe their point and efficiency to the long ones that have preceded them.

E. M. Bounds
Power Through Prayer

10
What Is Intercessory Prayer?

How Can I Learn to Pray for Others?

Throughout the previous pages we have referred to the term "intercession." To some people, this is a new concept, so I want to devote a chapter to enlarging upon this idea of intercessory prayer. Much of the remaining pages of the book will deal with the ministry of intercession. So, just what is intercession? We are told in the Old Testament that when the Messiah comes, He will "make intercession" for the transgressors (*see* Isaiah 53:12). Jesus was, and is today, the great intercessor. Hebrews 7:25 tells us that Jesus is this very moment living to intercede for us before the throne of God. The word *intercession* comes from a very old Greek word which was a technical term for one who approaches a king, thus it was used to describe prayer as approaching God. Our English word *intrude* comes from this Greek word. To intercede is to intrude upon someone in behalf of another. An intercessor is a "go between" who pleads the case of someone else. To intercede is to be a mediator.

A Special Kind of Prayer

Prayer takes many forms, but perhaps the praying that is closest to the heart of God is when we pray earnestly in behalf of others. Intercessory prayer is sacrificial prayer. It is not self-ish requests for personal wants, but rather it is prayer at its selfless best. Intercessory prayer can be a powerful weapon for good. It just may be the secret weapon of the church. I once heard intercessory prayer described as God's intercontinental ballistic missile. It can be aimed anywhere on earth; it always hits its target, traveling at the speed of thought. At times, it may even have a delayed detonation in that it may be answered years after it was "launched." The Lord Jesus launched a missile with your name on it nearly two thousand years ago, when in John 17:20 He prayed, "I do not ask in behalf of these alone, but for those also who believe in Me through their word." The day you were saved, God answered the prayer of Jesus prayed for you ages ago. What a tremendous weapon is intercessory prayer. I believe every time someone is born again, God has answered the prayer of Jesus again. Usually, when anyone is saved, it is in answer to an intercessor's efforts in prayer.

Storing Up a Legacy.   Parents, you have a secret weapon to use in defense of your children. When you pray for your children, you are storing up a history for that child. I personally have offered up prayers for my own children years ahead. When they were small, I prayed over their teenage years. This is planning for their future by putting God in their future. God will answer those prayers, years after I've prayed them. What's marvelous about this is that Satan has no weapon against this "stored up grace."

This is also true when we pray for a lost person. The lost person may not listen to you when you witness to him about God. He may not attend church with you or read the Bible you bought him. However, when you intercede for him and ask Jesus' Holy Spirit to knock on the door of that lost man's heart, Satan has no defense against your prayer. Jesus *will* go to that person and speak to him. Knowing this, should we not be launching our missiles daily? I fear the great sin of the modern church is our lack of intercession. We need the heart of Samuel the prophet who cried out, "Far be it from me that I should sin against the Lord by ceasing to pray for you" (1 Samuel 12:23).

A Parable of Intercession

Jesus told many wonderful stories, but none more simple and moving than the story of the persistent neighbor who comes knocking at midnight. Jesus told this parable to illustrate how God feels about intercessory prayer.

And He said to them, "Suppose one of you shall have a friend, and shall go to him at midnight, and say to him, 'Friend, lend me three loaves; for a friend of mine has come to me from a journey, and I have nothing to set before him'; and from inside he shall answer and say, 'Do not bother me; the door has already been shut and my children and I are in bed; I cannot get up and give you anything.' I tell you, even though he will not get up and give him anything because he is his friend, yet because of his persistence he will get up and give him as much as he needs. And I say to you, ask and it shall be given to you; seek, and you shall find; knock, and it shall be opened to you. For everyone who asks, receives; and he who seeks, finds; and to him who knocks, it shall be opened."

Luke 11:5–10

Bold Praying. If there is one central point to be learned from this story, it is the principle of boldness, daring, and authority! Here comes this very rude guy, banging on his neighbor's door at midnight. He just won't quit knocking until the head of the household awakens and comes to the door to meet his demands. How rude, how persistent, how very stubborn this intruder is. Our Lord's disciples have just asked Him to teach them to pray (*see* Luke 11:1). In this parable, Jesus is clearly saying, "Come to God's throne boldly. Be daring in your requests."

You Cannot Ask Too Much.   Our intercessions should be daring in the size of our requests. Notice the man comes and asks for *three* loaves, not just one. In those days, one loaf of bread was an entire day's supply of food! Amazing, yet that's how we are to come to God. Sadly, though, I've heard well-meaning people tell me you should not bother God with requests for "things." After all, God is too busy to bother with our everyday problems! Now, doesn't that sound spiritual? It may sound pious, but it is not biblical. I'm so glad our God isn't really like that. He wants us to ask big prayers. I've quoted it earlier in this book, but it needs to be shared again.

> Thou art coming to a king,
> Large petitions with thee bring;
> His grace and power are such,
> You can never ask too much.

Anything that is a genuine concern to you is of genuine concern to God. He wants to supply *all* your needs.

Bold and Stubborn.   The fellow comes knocking at midnight, and he is not only bold enough to ask for three loaves, he also is stubborn. He will not give up. In verse seven, Jesus says the head of the household will not come to the door until the man just keeps on knocking. "I tell you, even though he will not get up and give him anything because he is his friend, yet because of his persistence he will get up and give him as much as he needs."

Why did he give him as much as he needed? It had nothing to do with friendship. It was because of what the King James Version calls his "importunity." What in the world is importunity? This now less-familiar word was used to translate the Greek word for shamelessness. The New American Bible more accurately renders the word this way: The man was "shamelessly persistent"—he kept on knocking and finally, because of his persistence, the man arose from bed and gave him what he needed. This is how we are to repeatedly approach the throne of God in intercession. When praying for others—their salvation, protection, health, wealth, or whatever—Jesus said we are to ask and keep on asking, seeking, and knocking.[1] Then God will give it to us.

Begging a Reluctant God?   A natural question arises here. Are we trying to "pry" things out of the clenched fist of a reluctant God? No, not at all. We must remember, this is a special kind of praying we are dealing with here. We are interceding for others, in such praying, until God answers one way or another. At times, God waits to answer because there is much spiritual growth to be had in the struggle of prayer itself. Recall Jacob wrestling with the angel of the Lord at the brook called Jabbok (*see* Genesis 32:24–29). Throughout the night, Jacob struggled with this divine visitor. The angel pleads for Jacob to release him as dawn approaches. Jacob demands a blessing before he will release the angel. Reluctantly, the angel blesses Jacob, and Jacob releases this mysterious visitor. When one reads that passage, one gets the impression that there is something "fishy" about this all-night wrestling match. Since when can a man like Jacob wrestle with a mighty angel of God and pin him down and force a blessing out of him? It sounds to me as though that fight was fixed! I believe that angel was thoroughly enjoying the tussle. That angel was in no hurry to get loose. It was like a father wrestling with his little boy. It's as though the angel were saying to himself, "Hold on Jacob; I'm going to bless you if you'll just hold on a little longer."

Friend, God has much to teach us during our seeking, asking, and knocking. Our faith is stretched; our character is molded and hardened into persistence. What we learn in intercession is often more valuable than the answer. Praying for others builds humility and selfless love in us.

Intercession Demands Sacrifice. Another vital principle we see in the story is the sacrifice made by the man who comes knocking. At midnight, he goes out seeking food for his friend. His friend is hungry, but he has no means to feed him, so he totally identifies with his friend's hunger. He could have said, "If you are so hungry, you go out and wake up the neighbors, let them get angry with you." But he didn't do that. Instead, he so identified with the hunger of his friend that it became his problem. That is the heart of the intercessor: identification.

Have you ever felt that way for an unsaved friend? Has his lostness so consumed you that it became your burden? You put yourself in the place of that lost sinner and begin to carry his lostness in your very soul. His need is your need. I think of the great reformer, John Knox of Scotland, who cried out before the Queen of Scotland, "Give me Scotland or I die!" I see young David Brainerd kneeling down in the snow outside an Indian village, pleading to God to save the savages in those forests of New England during the years of 1743–47. Young Brainerd would pray for those Indians until he would faint from exposure and exhaustion. It took years of prayer and witness, but finally Brainerd broke through and God opened the doors of evangelism. His sacrifice broke his health and cost him his life, but David Brainerd became the first real missionary to that area, and his life has inspired thousands to a ministry of intercession and witness.

Real intercessory praying and living will demand the sacrifice of time, talent, even life itself. Only when we identify with the needs and hurts of others will we ever be prayer warriors for them. When we bleed, we bless; it can be no other way. May God give us the concern of Moses, who prayed, "Alas, this people has committed a great sin, and they have made a god of gold for themselves. But now, if Thou wilt, forgive their sin—and if not, please blot me out from Thy book which Thou hast written!" (Exodus 32:31, 32). That's the spirit of identification and sacrifice.

Desperate Praying. As we study further the subject of intercessory prayer, we'll see again and again the element of urgency in those who are true prayer warriors. The prayer warrior is often a desperate person. Indeed, the parable we are studying here just breathes urgency. The man comes at midnight, begging for food because he is desperate for help. He says, "a friend of mine has come to me. . . , and I have nothing to set before him" (Luke 11:6). The man had come to him and was his responsibility, and he took it seriously. I pray to God more Christians today would assume responsibility for the task God gives each of us! Parent, those children of yours are your charge to keep. God holds you responsible for their spiritual growth. It is not the church's job to raise your child. It is your inescapable responsibility. Your first and foremost privilege is to pray daily for your children. How God longs to hear parents pray for their children! Tragically, we often do not pray until trouble comes, and then it often is too late. Until we are desperate, we'll not pray urgent prayers.

The man in the parable was desperate because he had no food to give his visitor. Often, we do not pray faithfully because we think we have adequate resources within ourselves. As long as we have health, money, a job, or other material means, we tend not to depend on God. Just let those things evaporate, and we quickly discover our inadequate resources to cope with life. This is especially true in the spiritual realm. When we face problems that money and things cannot solve, then we are ready to pray. Believe me, the true intercessor *knows* that only God can meet the real needs of our lives. He knows "I have nothing" so he instinctively goes to his Heavenly Father, who has everything.

The Ministry of Intercession

Perhaps the greatest need in our world today is more and more true intercessors: people who believe in a God who answers prayers and who are willing to identify with a hurt and dying world; desperate people who will not let go of God until He blesses them and heals our world. In the pages to follow, we'll go even deeper into this ministry of intercession, which is so urgently needed.

Resources

1. "Keep on" asking, seeking, knocking correctly translates the sense of the present tense of the verbs.

Chapter 11

*Prayer is like an intercontinental
ballistic missile launched from the platform
of our life. The prayer is no more effective
than the life from which it issues. It's the
life that prays.*

Ronald Dunn
Lifestyle Ministries

11

Does Disobedience Hinder Your Praying?

What Is the Relationship Between Holiness of Life and Power in Prayer?

Does disobedience interfere with prayer? The answer to this question is so obvious, it seems redundant to consider it, yet it presents us with a topic that needs consideration. Far too often we are overly concerned with the content of our prayers, worrying if we are praying the right words, in the proper religious tone. We need to be reminded that God always looks beyond our words to the motive of the heart. Praying must always be more than words spoken to Deity. I've seen people write out beautiful public prayers, and oh, did they sound good. Is that necessary? Does the word choice and structure somehow greatly influence God? I think not. In fact, here is a spiritual principle worth learning: *It's the life that prays.* Always, first and foremost, it's the life that prays. The psalmist said it clearly: "If I regard wickedness in my heart, the Lord will not hear" (Psalms 66:18). The Lord Jesus stressed this principle in John 15:7 when He said, "If you abide in Me, and My words abide in you, ask whatever you wish, and it shall be done for you." You see, our "abiding" influences His answering. It's the life that prays.

Two Conditions for Answered Prayer

Did you ever wonder why some people's prayers seem to get ready answers and yours don't? Some people just seem to get through to God. Why is this? It seems to me that there are at least two key factors that govern God's answering our prayers.

First, the prayer request itself must be according to the will of God. First John 5:14 tells us this very clearly. No matter how much faith you have or how persistent you are, it will not help your prayer to be answered if you are not asking according to God's will.

Second, the person offering the prayer must be living according to God's will. God looks at the life of the one doing the praying. Prayer is launched, heavenward, from the platform of our life. It truly is the life that prays. The abiding influences the answering.

Quality and Acceptability. To some, this may sound strange, but in God's economy of things, the quality of the asker determines the acceptability of the prayer. Jesus emphasized this in the Sermon on the Mount. He said, "If therefore you are presenting your offering at the altar, and there remember that your brother has something against you, leave your offering there before the altar, and go your way; first be reconciled to your brother, and then come and present your offering" (Matthew 5:23, 24). Do you see how God looks at things? To Him, the quality of the giver is more important than the quality of the gift. The worshiper is more important than the act of worship. God looks at us before He considers the request. Many years ago, Robert Murray M'Cheyne said, "What a man is when he prays is what a man really is." I believe that's true, especially if you mean when we pray in private, not in public. In public praying, we tend to "fake it" at times. When we are alone with God in prayer, the real person shines through. Therefore, no man's personal life is greater than his prayer life. It really is the life that prays.

Disobedience and Praying. It is also true that when we are living in sin, we lose boldness and faith in prayer. A condemned heart cannot reach out in prayer. First John 3:20, 21 says, ". . . in whatever our heart condemns us; for God is greater than our heart, and knows all things. Beloved, if our heart does not condemn us, we have confidence before God." What happens when our heart condemns us because of sin? We lose fellowship with God, quench the Holy Spirit, and we lack the boldness to pray. Satan will come to you and lay a cloud of guilt over your head to keep you from looking upward. What a tragic state of affairs to lose precious prayer power over some petty sin—"If I regard wickedness in my heart, the Lord will not hear."

Wasted Lives and Unoffered Prayers. What a sad day, Christian, when at the judgment seat of Christ, Jesus tells you that there were people He wanted to save through your prayers, but because of some besetting sin of yours He couldn't pray through you. Your life so condemned you that the Holy Spirit could not intercede through you. My friend, nothing in all this world is worth losing power in prayer. James 5:16 says, "The effective prayer of a righteous man can accomplish much." Notice, it's the praying of a *righteous* man that gets the job done.

A Life Abiding

Returning to our Lord's words in John 15:7, "If you abide in Me, . . . ask whatever you wish, and it shall be done for you." Are you an "abiding" Christian? Are you living a life that is so abiding in Christ that He guarantees the answers to your prayers? To "abide" is to dwell, reside, or live in fellowship with someone. In this context, Jesus uses the figure of a branch and a vine. To abide in Christ means to be to Jesus what a branch is to the vine. The branch is totally available to the vine. It is dependent upon the vine for its life. The branch has only one purpose: to so abide in the vine that it must bear fruit.

If only you and I could be as unconditionally available to God as the branch is to the vine. Only heaven knows what fruits God would produce through us. Are you living a life that is unconditionally available to God for service and sanctification?

The Guilt Trip. There are times in my life when I feel really guilty because I am not doing more for Jesus. Maybe I have one of those days when I've neglected prayer, Bible study, or witnessing. Believe me—I have those days! Then I really feel lousy. I want to make up for it in a mad religious frenzy of "doing."

Suppose I come home and I have a conversation with the water faucet in my kitchen. I see a sad look on my faucet and I ask, "Faucet, why so blue today?" "Master, you haven't used me all day. I wanted to quench your thirst, wash your hands, help you wash the dishes, but you haven't turned me on all day." I reply, "You foolish water faucet, I could have turned you on any time I chose. I knew you were there and available. I don't want you turning yourself on; all you would do is waste water and probably make a mess of things." Okay, my point is, God has shown me that He is the vine, I am the branch. All I am to do is be unconditionally available. We are not to measure our faithfulness by our activity, but by our availability. However, to be truly abiding is not easy. To be unconditionally available to the Holy Spirit is the result of a life that is a broken vessel before God. That is one reason there are so very few real intercessors in the church today. True godliness comes from a yielded life.

Abiding in Jesus' Words. Our Lord mentions a second condition for answered prayer. "If you abide in Me, and My words abide in you, ask whatever you wish, and it shall be done for you." Notice, "and My words abide in you." There is a direct connection between our prayer life and our abiding in the Word of God. When the words of Jesus' teaching get into our spirit, some really exciting things begin to happen. Abiding in His Word means that Christ's Word begins to dwell permanently in you. Your heart has welcomed God's Word to dwell and abide there. As the Word gets into our hearts, it begins to control our behavior, shaping and guiding us.

For many of us, our heart is more like a hotel for the Word of God than a home. Checkout time is 12:00 noon on Sunday. An important question to ask yourself is: Does God's Word so permanently reside in my heart that it controls my life? That's what Jesus means by abiding in His Word.

Obedience and Prayer. As we abide in His Word, our praying becomes more effective: "And whatever we ask we receive from Him, because we keep His commandments and do the things that are pleasing in His sight" (1 John 3:22). Can you think of a commandment you are willfully disobeying? If so, your praying becomes ineffectual.

Holiness of life and fervent praying go hand in hand. Earlier, we spoke of the praying of David Brainerd, that early missionary to the North American Indian. E. M. Bounds, in his wonderful little book *Power Through Prayer,* says of Brainerd: "Let us often look at Brainerd in the woods of America, pouring out his very soul before God, for the perishing heathen, without whose salvation nothing could make him happy. Prayer—secret, fervent, believing prayer—lies at the root of all personal godliness."[1] Any time you see a man mighty in prayer, that man will also be mighty in the Word. The cleansing, controlling work of the Word will produce a life that will pray. Jesus said, "You are already clean because of the word which I have spoken to you" (John 15:3).

Pruning and Praying. God's Word in your life can so cleanse your life that God is able to empower you for service and prayer. Using the analogy of the vine and the branches, Jesus speaks of the pruning that is necessary for a healthy vine. Any vinedresser knows that to get a healthier vine, you do not add more branches, but, instead, you make the branches you already have healthier by pruning. Some of us have too much wood in our lives that needs God's pruning, cleansing work. The more He prunes, the more fruit we'll have in the future. Often, the necessary pruning and cleansing is not just the removal of sins, but the pruning out of so-called good things that can keep you from *God's* things. Television, sports, church, and a hundred other things can keep you from prayer. We can become so burdened with a busy schedule that there is no time for us to pray. The Heavenly Father may need to do some "clipping" on you to make time for effectual prayer.

Remember, it's the life that God considers. Are you willing to be the righteous man or woman He can use as an effectual, fervent prayer warrior? Can you be as available to God as the branch is to the vine? Saying, Father, I'll submit to the husbandman and allow You to prune, cut, and cleanse me until anything that hinders my life from praying is totally removed.

Resources

1. E. M. Bounds, *Power Through Prayer* (Grand Rapids, Michigan: Zondervan Publishing House, 1962), p. 24.

Chapter 12

Roots of Bitterness!

Nothing hinders prayer like unresolved conflicts. Anything that is an issue between you and your fellow man is an issue between you and your God. "See to it that no one comes short of the grace of God; that no root of bitterness springing up causes trouble. . . ."

Hebrews 12:15

12
The Greatest Hindrance to Answered Prayer

Must I Forgive in Order to Be Forgiven?

Because God looks at the life of the one making the request before He considers the request itself, it is crucial that we continually be living a life He can use. There are many hindrances to answered prayer. We have already discussed a number of them, such as sin or unbelief. However, the words of Jesus Himself in Mark 11:24–26, show that the failure to forgive is probably the greatest hindrance to answered prayer:

"Therefore I say to you, all things for which you pray and ask, believe that you have received them, and they shall be granted you. And whenever you stand praying, forgive, if you have anything against anyone; so that your Father also who is in heaven may forgive you your transgressions. [But if you do not forgive, neither will your Father who is in heaven forgive your transgressions.]"[1]

A Forgiving Spirit

These verses come as a shock to some people. Of all the things our Lord could have listed as hindrances to answered prayer, why does He stress lack of forgiveness? Several times in our Lord's teaching, He makes the point of showing how God feels about an unforgiving spirit. In verse 25, He reveals that a forgiving spirit is a prerequisite to answered prayer. It is obvious that anything that becomes an issue between you and your fellow man is also an issue between you and God. Our horizontal relationships are the key to our vertical relationship. We must be "right" with each other before God will even carry on a conversation with us!

Have you ever before considered that your power in prayer is conditional upon your relationships with other people? This is why the writer of Hebrews urges us to "Pursue peace with all men, . . . See to it that no one comes short of the grace of God; that no root of bitterness springing up causes trouble, and by it many be defiled" (Hebrews 12:14, 15). Nothing in all this world is worth losing power with God in prayer. Prayer is your lifeline. Therefore, anything that hinders prayer is just not worth the price. Because God will not forgive you if you do not forgive others, then you must never allow an unforgiving spirit to "bind" you up.

Continually Forgiving.   When Jesus commands us to "forgive" in Mark 11:25, the word He uses is in the present tense of the verb. It carries the idea of "be continually forgiving." Let forgiveness be your life-style, your manner of living. Do you carry a grudge against those who wrong you? Jesus says that if you do, you forfeit your right to pray. Nothing hinders prayer like bitterness and resentment. We must keep our forgiveness current. Make forgiveness the daily characteristic of your life. Why is this so important? Because you never know when you'll need to pray and need an immediate answer from God. When a child is taken ill and you need to be able to intercede for him, you don't have time to run all over the country, forgiving people and asking them to forgive you. You need to pray now! It's too late to "bury the hatchet" and stop resenting when an emergency arises. Our forgiveness must be current and continuous.

Deciding to Forgive. Often, people have said to me, "Barry, if you knew what that person did to me, you wouldn't ask me to forgive him. I just cannot forgive what he did to me." Well, what is forgiveness anyway? Some people have the mistaken idea that to forgive someone for a wrong means that you have to forget what they did to you and go on as though it never happened. This is not what forgiveness means. God does not say "forgive and forget." He just commands us to "forgive." The root idea of the word that Jesus uses here is to "send away, or get rid of." Thus, if I am to forgive you, I am to send away the emotion of hurt, bitterness, or resentment that I feel toward you. I cannot change the thing you did or said to me. That is history. It cannot be undone. However, I can change my response to it. This is what forgiveness is all about. *To forgive others is to make a volitional decision to rid myself of that feeling of hurt or resentment.* I decide to forgive you. I decide to "send away" that hatred and bitterness.

I once heard forgiveness defined as "tearing up your IOUs." An IOU is a slip of paper, signed by a debtor, indicating an indebtedness to be paid. The holder of the IOU has a lien on the debtor; he holds him "in debt." The indebtedness and the IOU is an issue between them. Forgiveness is tearing up your IOUs. Many of us hold IOUs on people. In our hearts, grudges, resentments, and hatred have built up over the years. These things are standing between us and true love and fellowship with those we have not forgiven. True forgiveness is when I tear up my IOUs—when I decide that the debt is paid; it is no longer an issue between us. Now, neither of us may ever be able to completely forget what happened, but we can determine that, as for how we will *respond* to the hurt, it is done and finished. This is forgiveness. This is what God requires between us. In that beautiful model prayer that Jesus taught us, He prayed, "And forgive us our sins, For we ourselves also forgive everyone who is indebted to us" (Luke 11:4).

Absolute Forgiveness. If you and I want fellowship with God and power in prayer, then we must be certain that there are no unresolved conflicts in our heart. Jesus said, "whenever you stand praying, forgive, if you have anything against anyone." Our Lord expects our forgiveness to be absolute and universal. We cannot pick and choose *whom* we will or will not forgive. Nor can we be selective as to *what* we will or will not forgive. Our forgiving is to be absolute as to the offense (anything) and as to the offender (anyone). This is very difficult to do. People hurt us, wound and abuse us. It is easier to resent conflict than to resolve conflict. We must remember, Jesus never said that continually forgiving others was easy. This going the "second mile" and forgiving "seventy times seven" is not for the weak and shallow of faith. Only those who have the love of God down deep in their souls can forgive absolutely and universally. "To err is human, but to forgive is divine."

A Delivering Force. A single woman recently told me the tragic circumstances of her divorce. Her ex-husband had really hurt her deeply. As I listened, my heart began to rage against this man who had treated his wife so cruelly. It was obvious why she hated him so. When I told her that she must forgive him, her eyes flashed with anger. "I can't," she replied. "Never! Never will I forgive him!" I took great pains to explain to her that the hatred in her was not hurting her ex-husband, but rather it was destroying her. Forgiveness benefits the one forgiving as well as the one forgiven. Hate, rage, anger, and rejection are negative, destructive forces in our lives. God wants to deliver us from these demons so that we can be healed and get on with the living of our lives. This is why God commands us to forgive. He doesn't just request it, He requires it. This is because He loves us and desires our own mental health and happiness. But more than that, He wants fellowship with us. He wants nothing to hinder that fellowship. He knows a man cannot love God, whom he has not seen, if he cannot love his brother, whom he has seen (*see* 1 John 4:20).

The Key to Peace. Forgiveness is the indispensable element in human relations. There can be no peace among men without it.

Often, we hear people say, "I'll forgive him if he says he's sorry. Whenever he asks for my forgiveness, he can have it." Have you ever felt like that? Listen, forgiveness is not passive; it is active. God teaches us that we are to forgive unconditionally. None of this, "if he says he's sorry" business. That's not how God deals with us, and it's not the way we are to relate to others. What a mess the world would be in if God had decided to wait for sinful man to "say he was sorry" before God chose to forgive us. Let's not forget that "while we were yet sinners, Christ died for us" (Romans 5:8). When we were not seeking God or His forgiveness, He unconditionally loved and forgave us. Christ died for His enemies! Forgiveness precedes repentance. Had God not demonstrated His great love for us, we would never have had the courage to believe we could ever be forgiven. The Son of God, dying on the cross, saying, "Father, forgive them"—that's what brings us back to God. That's the way we must love others. We forgive, whether they desire or seek our love and forgiveness. So many times I've seen it happen: when the offended one reaches out in love to the offending one, the offender's heart is changed and peace results.

One-Sided and Unconditional. "Whenever you stand praying, forgive. . . ." These are the strong words of the One who demonstrated it can be done. How precious to know that He who was "despised and rejected of men" has loved us and forgiven us. Following Christ's example, we are to give one-sided, unsought-for forgiveness. Whether those who offend us desire our forgiveness or not, we cannot afford to carry the offense in our breasts. We will send it away, rid ourselves of it, for peace of mind and peace with God.

The Results of Unforgiving

To demonstrate the tragic results of an unforgiving spirit, the Lord Jesus gave some vivid examples which illustrate this truth. The very fact that He places so much emphasis upon this subject tells us how crucial this issue is to God. Bitterness and resentment have at least a twofold tragic result.

Putting Yourself in Jail. One result of unforgivingness is taught in the Sermon on the Mount. In Matthew 5:23–26, Jesus states:

> "If therefore you are presenting your offering at the altar, and there remember that your brother has something against you, leave your offering there before the altar, and go your way; first be reconciled to your brother, and then come and present your offering. Make friends quickly with your opponent at law while you are with him on the way, in order that your opponent may not deliver you to the judge, and the judge to the officer, and you be thrown into prison. Truly I say to you, you shall not come out of there, until you have paid up the last cent."

What a graphic illustration! When you come to worship, and God reminds you that your brother has something against you (because you've done something to him!), Jesus says to go to him immediately and ask his forgiveness. What happens if you refuse to be reconciled? You, my friend, will put yourself in jail. That's right. In verses 25 and 26, Jesus concludes that if you do not agree with your adversary "quickly," then you'll put yourself in jail and won't come out until you pay your debt. What is the debt you owe? Forgiveness!

Surely you catch the meaning of this. Refusing to forgive or reconcile is such an issue between you and God that it keeps you away from God and puts you in spiritual prison. So many Christians are in spiritual bondage, refusing to pay what they owe. How tragic!

Putting Others in Jail. Jesus tells another story which illustrates another tragic result of people refusing to forgive:

> "For this reason the kingdom of heaven may be compared to a certain king who wished to settle accounts with his

slaves. And when he had begun to settle them, there was brought to him one who owed him ten thousand talents. But since he did not have the means to repay, his lord commanded him to be sold, along with his wife and children and all that he had, and repayment to be made. The slave therefore falling down, prostrated himself before him, saying, 'Have patience with me, and I will repay you everything.' And the lord of that slave felt compassion and released him and forgave him the debt. But that slave went out and found one of his fellow-slaves who owed him a hundred denarii; and he seized him and began to choke him, saying, 'Pay back what you owe.' So his fellow-slave fell down and began to entreat him, saying, 'Have patience with me and I will repay you.' He was unwilling however, but went and threw him in prison until he should pay back what was owed. So when his fellow-slaves saw what had happened, they were deeply grieved and came and reported to their lord all that had happened. Then summoning him, his lord said to him, 'You wicked slave, I forgave you all that debt because you entreated me. Should you not also have had mercy on your fellow-slave, even as I had mercy on you?' And his lord, moved with anger, handed him over to the torturers until he should repay all that was owed him. So shall My heavenly Father also do to you, if each of you does not forgive his brother from your heart."

Matthew 18:23–35

This parable is one of the longest and most detailed ever recorded in the gospels. It is very severe in tone. A wicked slave, who has been forgiven an enormous debt of ten million dollars by his master, has refused to forgive a fellow-slave a tiny debt of $18. He has that fellow-slave put in prison for that unpaid debt. What a thankless, unmerciful man this slave was! He has been forgiven, but he refuses to forgive others.

Sound like anyone you know? This hits close to home, doesn't it? When you refuse to forgive someone, you put that person in jail, which means you have so bound him up that he cannot be your friend. He cannot bless or help you because of your condemnation of him.

Getting Down on People.   This happens so frequently. Have you ever gotten down on someone over *nothing?* I mean nothing. You just get mad at that person and refuse to like or accept him, all because of some insignificant thing. You just make an "issue" over nothing. What happens? That person is in jail because you put him there. I've seen people do this with their pastor. The pastor does something you don't like. It may be nothing. Just something you don't agree with. Now, I ask you, can that pastor minister to you? Can he preach God's Word to you? Absolutely not! You've got him in jail! You have bound him up so that he cannot minister to you. He may know nothing about your feelings and be totally unaware he is in jail to you! How tragic! How we need to heed the words of Jesus: "So shall My heavenly Father also do to you, if each of you does not forgive his brother from your heart."

On Praying Ground.   May God teach us this great principle again and again: we cannot be right with God and be wrong with each other. When we won't talk to each other, God won't talk to us. Believe this, know this, do something about this. Let nothing hinder your position before God and your power in prayer. "When you stand praying, forgive!"

Resources

1. Verse 26 is enclosed in brackets or placed in the margin in The New American Standard Bible because it does not appear in several early manuscripts of Mark's gospel. However, Jesus teaches this principle elsewhere, as recorded in Matthew 6:15 and 18:35.

The great prayer problem of the modern church is not unanswered prayer, but unoffered prayer. "Ye have not because ye ask not."

13

When God Doesn't Answer My Prayers

Why Does God Not Answer, When I Think I'm Doing His Will?

Here is *the* most asked question regarding the subject of prayer: Why does God not answer, when I think I am doing His will? So frequently, even the most godly of saints goes to God in prayer, only to find that the Father just doesn't seem to hear. This can happen even when you are claiming a promise from Holy Scripture. Sometimes, all of the theology you've learned and all the attention you've given to praying "correctly" still does not produce *your* desired results. What do you do then?

Jesus told a prayer parable that I think lies at the heart of this question. It is recorded in Luke's gospel, chapter eighteen.

Now He was telling them a parable to show that at all times they ought to pray and not to lose heart, saying, "There was in a certain city a judge who did not fear God, and did not respect man. And there was a widow in that city, and she kept coming to him, saying, 'Give me legal protection from my opponent.' And for a while he was unwilling; but afterward he said to himself, 'Even though I do not fear God nor respect man, yet because this widow bothers me, I will give her legal protection, lest by continually coming she wear me out.' " And the Lord said, "Hear what the unrighteous judge said; now shall not God bring about justice for His elect, who cry to Him day and night, and will He delay long over them? I tell you that He will bring about justice for them speedily. However, when the Son of Man comes, will He find faith on earth?"

Luke 18:1–8

This story has always intrigued me, with its unjust judge who does not fear God nor respect man. He is a real scoundrel, yet he is a judge. He does not have a soft heart for widows, but when this persistent, stubborn widow just will not give up, he relents and, "lest she wear me out," meets her need and gives her justice before the law. What amazes me in this parable is that God is compared to this unjust judge. We are to be like the widow. We are to pray and not faint or lose heart. We are to keep coming before God in prayer with the same bulldog tenacity that this widow had before this cruel judge. Of course, God is unlike this judge in every way, except two: First, God honors persistence in prayer the way this cruel judge did who was worn out with her coming. Second, God will bring about "justice" when we persist and request it earnestly.

Keep On Keeping On. Many times, what we thought were prayers that God did not answer were prayers that ended too soon. We lacked persistence. We did not pursue justice as this stubborn widow did. This is true in praying for lost people. We are to pray *until* they are saved. This is true in praying for anything that is in line with God's revealed will in Scripture. Jesus said, "Shall not God bring about justice for His elect, who cry to Him day and night, and will He delay long over them?" (Luke 18:7). These words imply God's desire to answer and deal justly. However, there are circumstances in world affairs that require that God delay His reply and also require that His people tarry long in prayer.

Prayer and the Sovereignty of God. Not long ago, I was with a tour group in Israel, where we visited the Jewish Holocaust Museum. Several Jewish people in our group were very disturbed by the slide program showing the horrors of the Nazi concentration camps and the systematic extermination of the Jewish people. Some became very angry. As we talked in the lobby, one Jewish woman from Florida said to me, "Where was God when the Jews needed Him in Europe?" That's the kind of question that rocks us! Surely millions of dying Jews prayed to Jehovah God—their God. Where was the God of Abraham, Isaac, and Jacob? He allowed Hitler's madmen to brutalize His chosen people. Our heart cries out, "Why? Why? Why?"

Well, friend, hindsight is better than foresight. In fact, hindsight is "twenty-twenty," as a Texas friend of mine says. History has confirmed for us the sovereignty of God in His faithfulness to the Jewish people. He heard their prayers and delivered His people. He has dealt justice to the Jewish people. Some would question the accuracy of that statement, but it is true, nonetheless. God, in His permissive will, allowed the Holocaust to take place, to achieve His perfect will for the nation Israel. As we stood in the Holocaust Museum, I said to that angry Jewish woman, "Have you ever looked at it this way: if there had never been a Holocaust, there would never have been a nation Israel. Those Jews who survived in Europe had nowhere else to go; they were all but forced to go to Palestine. Now there is a national homeland for the Jewish people." She looked at me in wonder and said, "I never thought of it that way." I said, "God often works good out of evil, particularly when it fits His divine purpose to do so."

He Will Do Justly. As you and I ponder why God isn't working on our timetable, or why He doesn't answer our prayers the way we think He should, remember that God often sees the "big picture," while we see only the "little picture" of our own provincial world! He is looking through a wide-angle lens while we peep into a microscope. Our task is to believe that "Father knows best" and that He will always *do what's best.* We are to be like that widow coming before the judge, demanding "justice," but at the same time trusting and resting in His sovereign will. Jesus concludes this parable of the unjust judge by asking, "However, when the Son of Man comes, will He find faith on the earth?" (v. 8). In one sense, not all of our prayers for world peace, love, and brotherhood will be answered until the Son of Man comes. Then *every one* of those prayers will be answered! We must believe, keep the faith that His will is being carried out *in answer to our prayers.* We should "wear out" the judge of the universe who just happens to be our loving Heavenly Father!

A Final Word. Before closing this chapter, I offer one other word about unanswered prayer. There are other reasons why prayer is not answered or why the answer is a resounding "no" from heaven's throne. In another book, I wrote on the subject of unanswered prayer based upon James, chapter four.[1] In James we are told at least three other reasons why God doesn't answer our prayers. When it seems God isn't answering, look in three directions:

- *Look Outward.* Examine your prayer. James 4:3 says, "You ask and do not receive, because you ask with wrong motives, so that you may spend it on your pleasures." God cannot answer a wrong prayer with a right answer. Sometimes we are not praying according to His will.

- *Look Inward.* Examine your life. Sometimes the life is wrong. In James 4:4, he calls his readers "adulteresses." Remember, it's the life that prays.

- *Look Upward.* Look to God. He may be answering your prayer and you don't even realize it. He may either be delaying the answer or answering it differently than you expect.

Resources

1. See chapter 9 in *Questions New Christians Ask* (Old Tappan, New Jersey: Fleming H. Revell Company, 1979), pp. 93–102.

Chapter 14

What is evangelism? It is merely walking out on the battlefield after the war is won and picking up the spoils of war that were won in answered prayer.

14

Learning to Pray for Lost People

How Should I Pray for the Salvation of Others?

Have you been to church lately and heard a church leader conclude his public prayer, "Oh, yes, Lord, and if there are any unsaved people here today—save them all. Amen!" Such praying is very much like hearing a young child saying bedtime prayers, ". . . and God, save all the people in the world. Amen." Somehow, both of those requests leave something to be desired as concise, Spirit-led intercessions! Is there a special skill involved in praying for the salvation of others? I think there is. Not that anyone can't pray for the lost—anyone can. However, learning to pray with biblical understanding can greatly increase the effectualness of your interceding. A truth you can stand upon is that God desires to save the lost, and He anxiously awaits our prayers in their behalf.

A Reluctant God? Some people teach that God is not influenced by our praying. If this is so, then this book is a waste of time. Others feel that praying for the lost is a matter of begging a reticent, reluctant deity to arbitrarily save those for whom we plead. However, this is not the picture we see of God in Scripture. Just as Abraham interceded for Sodom until God was willing to save that wicked city if only ten righteous souls

133

could be found, so Jesus tells us He was sent by a loving Heavenly Father to seek and to save those who are lost. Paul describes God as the One "who desires all men to be saved and to come to the knowledge of the truth" (1 Timothy 2:4). The apostle Peter again affirms God's love for the lost when he writes that "The Lord is not slow about His promise, as some count slowness, but is patient toward you, not wishing for any to perish but for all to come to repentance" (2 Peter 3:9).

How to Pray for the Lost

Praying for the lost is a special kind of intercessory prayer. Those of us who pray for our unsaved friends should know that God is more willing to save the lost than we are to pray for them. We believe God is willing to save, and we stand on that promise. However, we must pray according to knowledge. We must use the tools that God has given us. He has given us the keys of the kingdom to set captives free. The job of "binding and loosing" is ours to perform. Praying for the lost is more than urging God. It is spiritual warfare in the truest sense. Therefore, we must deal with the devil as well as pray to our great God. Thus we will aim our prayer missiles in three directions: first, to launch a warhead toward Satan; second, to send a request to the Holy Spirit to release His convicting power; and, third, to deliver our petition before the mercy seat of God.

The Enemy and His Captive. Satan, our enemy, is target "A." He is the adversary who opposes the salvation of the lost. It is he who holds lost people captive. The condition of the lost sinner is such that Satan has both blinded and bound him. He is blind to the gospel and lives in spiritual darkness. He needs illumination to see the light of the gospel. He is also in chains, bound by the enemy, his will held captive. He needs to be emancipated.

The lost person is blinded to the truth: "... our gospel is veiled ... to those who are perishing, in whose case the god of this world has blinded the minds of the unbelieving, that they

might not see the light of the gospel of the glory of Christ . . ."
(2 Corinthians 4:3, 4). Furthermore, the lost person is a captive
slave to the enemy: ". . . if perhaps God may grant them repentance leading to the knowledge of the truth, and they may
come to their senses and escape from the snare of the devil,
having been held captive by him to do his will" (2 Timothy
2:25, 26).

What a horrible condition to be in! Our lost friends are like
we were—bound and blind. This ought to explain why the un-
believer is not interested in spiritual things. He is blinded to
truth. He just can't see it. First Corinthians 2:14 tells us that
spiritual things are foolishness to him. Only Jesus and the
power of the Holy Spirit can open his eyes to the truth. This is
why we must not condemn lost people. They are to be prayed
for, *not condemned.*

The unsaved person's eyes are blind and his will is bound.
He needs revelation—his mind is darkened, blinded. It is our
privilege and responsibility to help change his condition
through the power of intercessory prayer. Indeed, our witness
will be ineffective until the sinner's condition is changed. He
will not "hear" our words or decide for our Christ until he has
been delivered from Satan's control. Prayer that precedes
evangelism can change the condition of the lost.

The Victory. We are not to fret and hopelessly give up. Our
unsaved friends can be rescued. They have already been redeemed. Remember our teaching on Colossians chapter two.
The Lord Jesus has utterly defeated the devil; He has taken
away his only two weapons: our sins, and the wages of sin,
death. First John 3:8 tells us, ". . . The Son of God appeared
for this purpose, that He might destroy the works of the devil."

Our task is to use that mighty victory as our weapon in
prayer. Even though Satan has been defeated through the
death and resurrection of the Lord Jesus, the lost are still lost.
They are still captives. We must appropriate their deliverance
through intercessory prayer. Satan will not release them until
he is commanded to do so—in the name of the conquering

Christ. It is our daily, persistent resistance against him that will eventually drive Satan off the battlefield of the human heart and will. Let us again use the keys of the kingdom, our prayer weapons, and claim the lost for Christ. "For the weapons of our warfare are not of the flesh, but divinely powerful for the destruction of fortresses" (2 Corinthians 10:4).

Claiming Our IOU.   As you rebuke the devil, remember that you have every right to demand that he release your lost friend. Jesus has purchased this redemption for all men. The lost are no longer Satan's property. So, rebuke in faith and with authority, assaulting the gates of hell, demanding that Satan release the property that belongs to Jesus. Sign your command, "in Jesus' name." Satan must honor that IOU. Believe it! Claim it! Pray it!

One Other Word.   Praying for the lost is more than rebuking the enemy. It includes beseeching the throne of God. When I pray for the lost, I like to ask God for two things. Once I have driven the devil off the battlefield for that day, I daily ask God to send a witness to my friend. First, I ask Jesus Himself to go to that person. The Holy Spirit can and will go in your behalf upon your request. Ask Him, daily, to reprove, rebuke, and convict the sinner of his need. Second, I ask God to send someone into my unsaved friend's life to share the gospel with him. It may be a television gospel show, a gospel tract he picks up, it may be a stranger who will share with him. That's God business, but we can ask Him to send forth laborers into the harvest (*see* Matthew 9:38).

Now, all of this is not that complicated. It's only a matter of praying "according to knowledge." Let me give you a suggested outline for interceding for the lost.

1. *Rebuke the adversary.* Pray, "Satan, I come against you in behalf of my friend _____. In the name of Jesus the Christ, I command you to loose him today. You have

no right to him. He belongs to the Lord Jesus, and I am claiming his salvation in Jesus' name."

You must do battle day after day until salvation comes. Take heart; when Satan realizes you mean business, he will back off. However, he will not obey if your faith is weak and your intercessions are not continuous.

2. *Request the Holy Spirit to convict.* Ask Jesus to come to your friend this day. Pray, "Lord Jesus, I ask You to knock on his heart. Show him Your love; open his eyes to the truth. Speak to him today."

3. *Request God to send believers.* Pray, "Father, send a witness today to my friend. Surround him with Your love. Bring some human influence into his life that will bring him closer to You."

4. *Thank God for his salvation.* Claim 1 John 5:14. Believe your friend *is being saved.* Thank the Father in advance for saving your friend. Leave the *when* and *how* up to God. Let God do it His way and in His own time—but ask and keep on asking, knock and keep on knocking, and the lost will be saved.

The true intercessor has learned and lived the law of Spiritual Harvest: life comes forth out of death. "Except a grain of wheat fall into the ground and die it abideth alone: But if it die, it brings forth much fruit."

John 12:24

15

How Can I Become an Intercessor?

Almost forty-five years ago, Dr. S. D. Gordon penned these words of challenge:

> The great people of earth today are the people who pray. I do not mean those who talk about prayer; nor those who say they believe in prayer; nor yet, those who can explain about prayer; but I mean these people who *take* time and pray. These are the people today who are doing the most for God; in winning souls; in solving problems; in awakening churches; in supplying both men and money for mission posts; in keeping fresh and strong these lives far off in sacrificial service on the foreign field where the thickest fighting is going on; in keeping the old earth sweet awhile longer.[1]

What a wonderful paragraph! Did you notice that it is the intercessor who is "keeping the old earth sweet awhile longer"? Not government, education, culture, or anything else man might achieve; only vital intercession truly "sweetens" this old planet. Do you really want to be one of those great people whom God uses in prayer to hammer out His eternal purposes on earth? Not just reading about prayer, or talking about prayer, but really praying?

As we have discussed earlier, prayer can take many forms. It can be simply *communion* with God the Father. Prayer as communion is the truest form of worship. It is meeting God in the quiet place, just to be with Him, to praise and adore Him; even just to listen for the still, small voice that can make each day a God-directed day. Second, prayer may be *petitioning* the Father. Prayer, often, is asking God for your own needs. It is the sinner humbly asking God for his daily bread, for forgiveness or strength. Prayer can be communion and petition, but it also can be *intercession.* Intercession is the highest form of service that one person can render to another. Those who enter the ministry of intercession have entered the Holy of Holies, where God lives. To be an intercessor is to identify with Christ in His love and compassion for a lost and dying world. Communion prayer is subjective—*it affects me.* Prayer as petition is also subjective—*its reach is within.* However, intercession is the objective outward influence of prayer—*it affects a world!*

S. D. Gordon calls intercession the climax of prayer.[2] By that, he means that through our communion with God (worship) and our petition, God is able to so reach us that through us He is able to reach a world. Through communion and petition, God fills a life with power. This power then manifests itself in a life given over to praying for others. We cannot be an intercessor without first having been to the mountaintop to meet God. Having met God, a man will share God's passion to reach a world lost in sin, because God Himself is interceding for our world. To be close to God is to share His burden for the wayward planet. Those who enter into the ministry of intercession are those who "have seen a great light" and it has illuminated their very soul to see a world in darkness.

Becoming an Intercessor

Can just anyone become an intercessor? The answer, it seems to me, is both yes and no. When we look at Scripture, we are taught to pray for others. Paul tells us to pray "... on behalf of all men, for kings and all who are in authority, . . ." (1 Timothy 2:1, 2). In a sense, any Christian can and should pray for "all men." The intercessory prayer is to be a part of every faithful Christian's life-style. Yes, every Christian can be an intercessor. However, not many Christians will ever become prayer *warriors,* living truly committed lives yielded to God for the *ministry* of intercession. There are those few choice souls who will become so identified with our Lord for a lost world that intercession becomes their life calling. This calling is not for the faint of heart or weak of faith.

A Select Group. The ministry of intercession is a very select "club." Its membership is restricted, yet among its membership are both the famous and the unknown. Moses was a charter member of this select group. What a life Moses offered to God! Moses "stood in the gap" for an entire nation. He was willing to give his life, if it would stay the hand of God's anger against the rebellious Israelites. Praying with his life on the line, he pleads, "Oh, this people have sinned a great sin, and have made them gods of gold. Yet now, if thou wilt forgive their sin—; and if not, blot me, I pray thee, out of thy book which thou hast written" (Exodus 32:31, 32 KJV). Moses was an intercessor. Paul, the beloved apostle, qualifies for membership. Paul carried the burden of a lost Jewish nation upon his shoulders. He confesses in Romans, "Brethren, my heart's desire and my prayer to God for them is for their salvation" (Romans 10:1). "I am telling the truth in Christ, I am not lying, my conscience bearing me witness in the Holy Spirit, that I have great sorrow and unceasing grief in my heart. For I could wish that I myself were accursed, separated from Christ for the sake of my brethren, my kinsmen according to the flesh" (Romans 9:1–3). There it is again—a man who is so identified with the lostness and hurt of others that he would gladly lay down his life for them. This is the very heart of intercession, the climax of prayer. Paul was a great intercessor. In Acts 20:31, he reminds the Ephesians that "night and day for a period of three years I did not cease to admonish each one with tears." Paul was many things—teacher, missionary, apostle, writer, and evangelist. However, these all were secondary to what he truly was—an intercessor.

Jesus the Intercessor. This is as it should be. Those who follow the Master begin to become like Him. Jesus is an intercessor. Centuries before Jesus the Messiah was born, the prophet Isaiah described the Messiah as an intercessor, "Therefore, I will allot Him a portion with the great, and He will divide the booty with the strong; because He poured out Himself to death, and was numbered with the transgressors; yet He Himself bore the sin of many, and interceded for the transgressors" (Isaiah 53:12). Jesus our Lord was that promised Messiah. He was truly the great intercessor. All of His life was an intercession: living, loving, praying, and dying for others. In Luke 22:32, Jesus prays for Simon Peter, whom he knew was going to betray Him. He said, "Simon, I have prayed for you, that when you are converted, you will feed My sheep" (author's paraphrase). In John 17, we find what we actually could call the Lord's Prayer, for it is, in reality, the prayer of our Lord for His disciples. The entire seventeenth chapter of John is a high priestly intercession by Christ in the behalf of His church. He is interceding for His disciples and for all of us who would be saved down through the centuries as a result of their witness.

Jesus prayed for you, my friend, and Jesus prayed for me. He was an intercessor, not only in His life but in His death as well, for He was numbered with the transgressors and made intercession for them. As He was dying on the cross, Jesus prayed to God, "Father forgive them; for they know not what they do" (Luke 23:34 KJV)—our great intercessor, praying for others, even as He died on the cross. Did you know that Jesus Christ is an intercessor right now at the right hand of God? The writer of the book of Hebrews, in chapter seven, verse twenty-five, makes this statement about the Lord Jesus, "He is able to save forever those who draw near to God through Him since He always lives to make intercession for them." In other words, at this very moment, the activity that preoccupies the mind of Christ is the activity of intercessory prayer. Jesus is praying on our behalf at this very moment. He lives for the very purpose of interceding for us. How incredible! Jesus lives to intercede. Jesus is *the* intercessor.

Lives and Lips

Now, are you in the habit of faithfully praying for other people? I have discovered that the ministry of intercession and intercessory praying is a very difficult thing to do, for we are basically self-centered people. Intercessory praying is the result of intercessory living. It comes from identifying with another person's hurt. Parents will pray for their child because they care about the child; and if you and I care enough about other people to identify with them in their pain, then we will pray for other people. So intercessory praying is the result of involved intercessory living.

Identification: Moses prayed the way he did because he was totally identified with the people of Israel. The Hebrew children, wandering across the deserts of Sinai, were Moses' personal responsibility. He identified with their transgression, their rebellion, and their need, so he prayed for them. The Lord Jesus prayed for you and me, because as the Messiah Savior, Scripture says, He was numbered with the transgressors. That simply means that Jesus was totally identified with the sin of humanity. In His baptism (*see* Matthew 3:13–17), when Jesus the sinless Son of God came to John the Baptist and requested to be baptized, John, in all sincere humility, said, "Master, You come to me? I have need to be baptized of thee." But Jesus said, "Allow it to be so, John, for thus it becomes us to fulfill God's righteousness." Now, what Jesus was doing in His baptism was identifying Himself with the sins of humanity. He was so close to the sinner that His baptism is a symbol of

His total identification. It was representative of His death on the cross, when He would take our sins upon Himself. First Peter 1:18, 19, says we are justified, not with the perishable things, such as silver and gold, but with the precious blood of Jesus Christ.

Intercessory praying is the by-product of intercessory living. The life controls the lips. Until I identify with others in their need, I will not pray for them. I can remember when I was a college student, a tragedy occurred that shook the evangelical world. Several missionaries were martyred in South America. One of those young men who died at the hands of the Indians with whom he was trying to share God's love was Jim Elliot. When Jim Elliot was a student at Wheaton College near Chicago, Illinois, he kept a diary. He had a great heart for missions. It was the burden of young Jim Elliot's life that he become a missionary and that he go and share Christ with a people who had never heard the name of Jesus. Jim Elliot and his friend, Nathaniel Saint, heard about a tribe of Indians in the jungles of Peru who had never heard of Jesus Christ. Long before he ever went to South America, Jim Elliot began to pray daily in his diary, asking God to allow him to go and tell these forgotten people about his Savior. One day Jim wrote, "God, make of me a crisis man, bring those I contact to decision, let me not just be a milepost on a single road, but make me to be a fork, that men must turn one way or another, having faced Christ in me."[3] Jim Elliot was an intercessor, in that his life was identified with the hurt and lostness of a whole tribe of people. Finally, this prayer burden was translated into action as he gave his life to share the gospel with the Quechua Indians.

Intercessory praying is the result of intercessory living. That is, you are not going to have a ministry of intercessory prayer until your life is a ministry of caring for others. If you are not willing to be involved in the hurt, the need, the pain of other people, then you certainly aren't going to pay the price to pray for other people.

More Than Prayer. The ministry of intercession is open to all who will seek it and pay the price for it. However, a ministry of intercession is not to be confused with just intercessory praying. Norman Grubb, in his foreword to *The Intercession of Rees Howells*[4] quotes Howells as saying (during a crisis time of World War II), "Prayer has failed and only intercession will take us through." Notice the distinction—intercession is more than prayer. How many times have you and I tried to stir up a concern for people, and we temporarily get involved in ministry or temporarily get out a prayer list and pray for people, only to find that we would soon lay it aside and become indifferent and that we could not sustain that high spirit of concern and compassion in prayer? Intercession is a life-style, not a temporary burden or an occasional concern. Intercession is the result of a broken heart. It is the result of walking in the Spirit, and abiding in Christ.

In Zechariah 12:10, the Holy Spirit is called the Spirit of intercession or the Spirit of supplication. In other words, it is the very nature of the Spirit of Christ who indwells the believer to pray in behalf of other people. He *is* the Spirit of intercession. In Romans 8:26, the Scripture says that the Holy Spirit Himself intercedes for us on our behalf, with groanings that cannot be uttered by the human tongue or heart. Now listen, the Holy Spirit *is* the intercessor. Jesus, when He was here on this earth, lived an intercessory life in behalf of sinners, He died an intercessory death, and He prayed intercessory prayers. Now when Jesus Christ is abiding in us and is allowed to control our inner being, then His nature becomes our nature, and we receive from Him this intercessory heart and this intercessory life-style. Because Jesus ever liveth to intercede, then when He lives in us and when we are yielded in obedience to His Spirit, we can have this intercessory ministry.

Rees Howells and John Hyde. In the history of the church, there have been those people who have been so identified with a ministry of intercession that their very name speaks of this ministry. John Hyde spent his life in India as a missionary. So great was his burden for the lost and so great was his prayer life that he became known as "Praying Hyde." It was said of John Hyde that, "He proved that prayer was an evangelical force in India when, by faith, he claimed one soul a day, then two, then four."⁵ Such, too, was the life-style of Rees Howells of the Bible College of Wales. Heaven alone knows the impact of the prayer warfare of Rees Howells. Just mention his name to those who know anything about a praying church and they'll tell you Rees Howells was an intercessor. Although he died in 1950, the impact of his life and prayers will continue for eternity. My friend, intercession is a high road, and few, very few, can walk it. The air is too thin up there for most of us. If you desire to become an intercessor, you must so become one with Christ that His Spirit has control of your life. This is the secret. Intercessory living is the result of abiding in Christ. When you and I find ourselves caring about people, praying for people, even being willing to sacrifice time and other activities in order to pray, then it is because Christ is interceding through us.

The Intercessor Knows Victory

When we are abiding in Christ, it is also true that you and I can have the assurance that our prayers are going to be answered. The intercessor is able to ask and claim ground for God. He is a mediator, fighting for God and man. The intercessor takes the place of the one he is praying for. He feels for, aches for, the one for whom he prays. He is standing in the gap. He will stand there, doing warfare until he knows he has won the victory. If we abide in Christ and His words abide in us, we can know that what we ask will be given (John 15:7). The intercessor stands on this firm ground with God and His Word.

May God grant to His church more and more folks who can pray like that. The door to intercession is open to all who have the courage to walk in and claim this ministry. Many hundreds of churches continue, week after week, year after year, and there is not one true intercessor among the membership. How desperate this situation really is. Where are those who are willing to pray until the Lord of the Harvest comes? Are there people that you are praying for on a consistent daily basis? Is there anyone for whom you share such an overwhelming burden that your heart cries out, "God help this person, or I think I'll die"? Have you ever just totally "stood in the gap" for anyone? The ministry of intercession is for those who will take up another's burden and carry it.

I personally thank God almost daily for those faithful few who pray for me and the worldwide ministry God has given me. There have been many times when I have felt the prayers of God's people upon me as I preach, minister, and witness literally around the world. Recently, I traveled three weeks behind the Iron Curtain, ministering in Hungary, Romania, Czechoslovakia, and Poland. Frequently, we were in very difficult situations, followed by the secret police, under police harassment or surveillance. So many times, we have seen the power of God come down in miraculous answers to prayer. At very difficult communist border crossings, God protected us and got us through. Many friends were daily standing in the gap for us. Their prayers paved a highway for us.

I believe in the ministry of intercession. I believe that God honors the prayers of a Spirit-filled believer and that when a Christian is yielded to Christ, abiding in Christ, *that* Christian can affect his world and touch his world. He can bring God into the fight, through the power of intercessory prayer. I would to God that He could call you out, dear reader, to a life of intercession. You can have a supernatural prayer ministry that will change your world. Your prayers can make *the* difference. Together, interceding, we can "sweeten this old world" till Jesus comes.

Resources

1. S. D. Gordon, *Quiet Talks on Prayer* (Grand Rapids, Michigan: Baker Book House, 1980), pp. 13, 14.

2. Ibid., p. 43.

3. Elisabeth Elliot, *Through the Gates of Splendor* (Wheaton, Illinois: Tyndale House Publishers, 1981).

4. Doris M. Ruscoe, *The Intercession of Rees Howells* (Fort Washington, Pennsylvania: Christian Literature Crusade, 1983), p. 9.

5. Francis McGaw, *Praying Hyde* (Minneapolis, Minnesota: Bethany Fellowship, 1970), p. 9.

Chapter 16

*How can we recover apostolic power
while neglecting apostolic practice? How can
we expect the power to flow if we do not prepare
the channels? Fasting is a God-appointed means
for the flowing of His grace and power.*

Arthur Wallis
God's Chosen Fast

16
What Is Fasting and Its Relation to Prayer?

What is fasting? Does it have any rightful place in the life of modern, twentieth century Christianity? My guess is that at least 95 percent of the people who are reading these words have never experienced even one twenty-four hour period of scriptural fasting. Very few believers today have any real understanding about the ministry of prayer and fasting.

A Forgotten Subject

In my own personal experience, I must say that any Bible teaching on prayer and fasting was a totally neglected subject in the churches I attended as a youth. I have no remembrance of the subject ever being taught or practiced among Christians that I knew. In truth, the first person I ever met who practiced fasting was a rather strange, "way out" street preacher, Arthur Blessitt.

Chained to a Cross. In the spring of 1969, I became pastor of the First Baptist Church of Beverly Hills, California. Those were the days of the youth explosion that later became known as the hippie movement. Sunset Strip in West Hollywood, California, was the gathering place for thousands of runaway youth. My little church was just a few hundred yards from Sunset Strip. It was there on the street, witnessing to these misguided young people, that I first encountered Rev. Arthur Blessitt. Arthur ran a Christian "coffeehouse" type ministry on Sunset Strip. His life and ministry touched thousands of lives for God.

In the midst of this great ministry, Arthur's lease on his building was revoked. The owner of the building wanted Arthur and his strange Christian army out of his property and off Sunset Strip. Christians witnessing for Jesus were bad for business, especially when your business happened to be prostitution, drugs, homosexual bars, strip joints, and such. A property owner's cartel was formed, and none would rent a suitable building to Arthur Blessitt. It was during this turbulent time that I learned about seeking God through prayer and fasting. In protest against his being evicted from his coffee house ministry, Arthur Blessitt chained himself to an eight-foot cross and sat down on the sidewalk in front of a famous teenage night club, "The Whiskey à Go-Go." There he sat, a cross leaning against a telephone pole, with a chain around it, and the other end of the chain locked to his own wrist. There he sat, witnessed, prayed, and fasted for twenty-eight days! During that time, he ate no foods and drank only water and juices.

My initial reaction was typical—I thought he was crazy! I questioned his motives and methods. It looked like a "showbiz" play for publicity to me. It did gain much publicity! Worldwide publicity was turned Arthur's way during those four weeks. He lost a pound of body weight for every day he fasted. Sitting in the hot California sun every day was an exhausting experience. However, God was in it. Great spiritual results were obtained. As crowds gathered to come and look at the "Jesus freak," many hundreds came to know Christ; Christians rallied around Arthur, supporting his protest. God was honored, and lives were changed. One of those lives that was changed was my own.

Search the Scriptures.   It was this experience on the street with Arthur that forced me to go back to my Bible and see what God had to say on this subject of fasting. My research overwhelmed me! I was amazed that I had overlooked this vital teaching. One cannot live a life of prayer and intercession without the ministry of fasting. If you doubt me, then I challenge you to just look in any Bible concordance for the words *fast* or *fasting.* It will shock you to see how much God includes this ancient practice as a normal part of the obedient Christian's life-style. In this chapter, I want to share with you what I have discovered about fasting and prayer.

What Is Fasting?

We must not assume that everyone even understands what we mean by the term *fasting.* Some think fasting is dieting! Others think fasting is only ancient asceticism and has no place in the modern church. Okay, just what do we mean when we urge believers to "fast and pray" (*see* Matthew 17:21)? The Old Testament Hebrew word literally means to "cover the mouth." I know some overweight folks who could stand a few days of "covering the mouth." The New Testament Greek word means "not to eat," or to abstain from eating. However, fasting is more than not eating for a stated period of time. It might be helpful to describe fasting in two categories—the secular fast and the spiritual fast.

The secular fast could take one of two forms. It could simply be dieting to lose weight for health purposes; there are many doctors who know the physical benefits of such fasting. Doctors often prescribe a partial fast for a patient. Fasting may include not eating certain foods for a period of time for health reasons. Some people mistakenly think fasting is starving oneself to death. They see it as an unhealthy, negative thing to do. Nothing could be further from the truth. Certain kinds of fasting have great health benefits. Fasting helps to purify the body of excess wastes and impurities. When the stomach and colon are emptied, the body then begins to feed upon itself, removing first of all those wastes, impurities, fats, and so on, that the healthy body does not need. Fasting as a secular practice can have tremendous health benefits, especially when supervised by a doctor or health nutritionist. Even a simple twenty-four-hour fast, drinking only water, can destroy sluggishness, give vitality to your life, and free your spirit for spiritual activities. We'll talk more about the spiritual benefits of fasting later.

Asceticism and the Bible.   Another type of secular fast may be religious in nature, but it is not the same as the scriptural fast we are about to discuss. For many pagans, religious fasting is an integral part of worship. The pagan worshiper fasts to mortify the body to gain the favor of his deity. This may include actually harming the body (nails, pins, and so on) as an act of worship. Now, this is not biblical fasting. The body is not an evil thing that needs to be punished. In God's Word, fasting is always done for spiritual reasons. We go without food or water (or both) because we are seeking deeper fellowship with God. A scriptural fast is not dieting to lose weight, nor is it to punish the body. Granted, a Christian may be overweight, and fasting can be a call from God to seek freedom over slavery to physical appetites. Biblical fasting always has a spiritual rather than a secular motive.

Why Should I Fast?   Many Christians have gone to church for years, lived what they consider to be a normal Christian life and have never entered into covenant with God to fast. The obvious question arises, "Why should I fast?" It might be helpful if I made some suggestions as to why fasting (not eating) may be necessary for every believer from time to time. We have all heard the expression that the way to a man's heart is through his stomach. This statement is truer than we might think. Our physical appetites are the door to the heart. The five senses are the avenues through which we reach the soul. Satan knows this better than we do. Throughout the Bible, we see Satan reaching a man's heart through that man's stomach. He reached Eve in the Garden of Eden through her physical appetites. Genesis records that she saw that the fruit was good to eat. The fall of the original couple was through their physical senses. The body is the doorway to the soul. Again, Satan used this approach with Noah after the flood. Genesis 9 tells us that Noah became drunk from the wine of his vineyard and his sons found him in his nakedness. It was a sin of physical appetite that defeated Noah. Again, recall Esau and Jacob, the sons of Isaac. Esau sold his birthright to his brother for a bowl of soup! Satan uses the physical appetites to reach the soul and spirit of a man. Now, what does this have to do with fasting? Everything! The Bible teaches us that the physical appetites are from God and not evil in and of themselves. It is the misuse and abuse of the body that is sinful. We must discipline and control our physical desires. We "subdue" the body and make it our servant so that our spirit rules the body, not vice versa.

In the Wilderness. In Matthew 4, it is recorded that the Lord Jesus fasted forty days and nights in the desert. For these forty days He ate no food. After this period of time, the Bible declares, "then He became hungry." It was then that Satan came to tempt our Lord. What appeal did Satan make first? The enemy tempted Jesus to turn stones into bread—an appeal to His fleshly need for food! However, Jesus' fasting had made Him "mighty in spirit." The body was His servant. Our Savior was hungry, but for Him the way to His heart was *not* through His stomach. What I want us to understand is that there is a very definite relationship between a man's physical appetites and his spiritual life. How you discipline your body often reflects your spiritual discipline. (This is not always true, of course.) Fasting is one means of breaking the "hold" that physical desires have over our will.

It's Not for Me. By now it should be clear that fasting is indeed beneficial and taught in Scripture. Why, then, do so few of us practice fasting as a part of our Christian experience? You may be like an overweight preacher friend of mine who adamantly declared, "It's not for me!" Well, why not? Briefly, let me suggest some reasons fasting is neglected today:

- *Legalism.* Some are afraid fasting will become a religious tradition or law that you *must* do. They see it as putting people under law and not grace. Many people are just afraid of that kind of bondage. Why is it that we feel that way about fasting, when we don't feel that way about prayer, witnessing, or tithing? Any Christian activity can become legalistic, can't it? Tithing can become legalistic, but we evangelicals sure haven't neglected the teaching of tithing!

- *Asceticism.* Second, it's been neglected for fear of asceticism. During the Middle Ages, when the Roman Catholic Church began to emphasize asceticism, the monastic life, the cloistered life, fasting became a very real part of asceticism. Just what is asceticism? The ascetic often is one who mortifies his body, who buffets his body; it's the idea of subduing the body, torturing the body, or punishing the body for spiritual reasons. Many pagan religions today are ascetic in nature. One occasionally reads of somebody who has either been sticking pins in his body and fasting, or starving himself to death, in order to gain the favor of his god. I think, perhaps, many modern Christians have rebelled against that kind of fanaticism and that kind of extremism. But fasting in the Bible is not asceticism.

- *Liberalism.* Third, I feel fasting is being neglected simply because some preachers and teachers have taught that fasting does not apply to us today. Some say it belongs to ancient Judaism but is not a part of the Christian experience in our day. However, if you'll look at your Bible, all of the great saints of God in the Scriptures fasted as well as prayed, witnessed, and preached.

Old Testament Intercessors. It is remarkable to me that Moses, the greatest man of the Old Testament, is also our greatest example of the connection between prayer, intercession, and fasting. Moses is the prime example of an intercessor who used fasting as a means of spiritual communion. On two occasions, Moses fasted forty days, going without food or water. Such a thing is physically impossible without supernatural intervention. Moses actually went eighty days without food or water. A man will die if he has no water after about fifteen days. What Moses did is miraculous. Scripture tells us that Elijah fasted forty days. Queen Esther fasted for three days and nights, pleading with God to spare the Jews from the edict of her king. All of the biblical saints—David, Nehemiah, Ezra, Daniel, Jeremiah, and Isaiah, to name a few—were men and women who practiced fasting along with prayer and intercession.

Jesus' Teaching on Fasting

In the Sermon on the Mount, Jesus gives us basic teaching regarding the practice of fasting. In Matthew 6, Jesus deals with three great religious duties—almsgiving, prayer, and fasting. It is here that our Lord speaks of the abuse of these things. In Matthew 6:2–4, He talks about the giving of alms, or giving money or gifts to the poor:

"When therefore you give alms, do not sound a trumpet before you, as the hypocrits do in the synagogues and in the streets, that they may be honored by men. Truly I say to you, they have their reward in full. But when you give alms, do not let your left hand know what your right hand is doing that your alms may be in secret; and your Father who sees in secret will repay you."

Jesus teaches the same principle about giving. He says, "when you give." It is Christian to give, right? Jesus did not say, *if* you give; He assumed that we would give to the poor. He says, "*when* you give"; then He tells you how to do it. He says don't boast about it; don't do it in public; do it in secret; and do it just for the sake of doing it, not for the glory that will come to you.

Then, in Matthew 6:5–15, Jesus talks about prayer. Now prayer is a God-given ministry. Praise the Lord for the ministry of prayer! But prayer can be abused, and Jesus talks about the abuse of prayer. He talks about the model prayer that is given to us at the beginning of verse nine. He says, when you pray, pray this way: "Our Father who art in heaven, . . ." and He describes the model prayer. Through verse fifteen, He talks to us about praying and forgiving others lest our Father not forgive us. Jesus assumed that the Christian would pray. He didn't say *if* you pray; he said, "*when* you pray."

Now, the third religious duty that He talks about is found in verses 16–18. That duty is fasting!

"And whenever you fast, do not put on a gloomy face as the hypocrits do, for they neglect their appearance in order to be seen fasting by men. Truly I say to you, they have their reward in full. But you, when you fast, anoint your head, and wash your face so that you may not be seen fasting by men, but by your Father who is in secret; and your Father who sees in secret will repay you."

Now let me show you what is significant about that. Jesus said, "*when* you give," "*when* you pray," and "*when* you fast." The question isn't *if* you should fast; the question is *when* you fast. You can readily see that Jesus put fasting in the same category with praying and giving.

Now, I don't think that we have any question today that a Christian ought to give. There is no question that a Christian ought to pray. Then why is it that we have questioned this matter of fasting? Why have we rejected it? Jesus said, *"when* you fast" not *if* you fast. He assumed that the believer would make fasting a part of his Christian ministry and his Christian experience. Jesus assumed we would do something most of us are not doing!

Some people have said, "Well, was the Sermon on the Mount meant for all believers of all times?" There are those who have said you cannot take the teachings of the Sermon on the Mount because that was before Pentecost, and it represents the old dispensation of the law. They point out that the Sermon on the Mount is very Jewish, and that Jesus is talking to Jewish believers. Therefore, they say, this passage on fasting isn't for today. I do not accept that explanation because I believe the Sermon on the Mount is timeless—it applies to all true believers in Christ.

However, Jesus taught us elsewhere about the place of fasting in the life of the church. In Matthew 9:14 we read, "Then the disciples of John [the Baptist] came to Him, saying, 'Why do we and the Pharisees fast, but Your disciples do not fast?" Now the Pharisees fasted twice a week. They were not commanded by God to fast twice a week; in fact, there is only one commandment in the Word of God to fast, and that's on the Day of Atonement, Yom Kippur. That's the only fast that God declared. But the Pharisees had become so legalistic about it, they were fasting twice a week, and they had abused the biblical injunction where fasting is concerned. Also, the followers of John the Baptist were fasting, but the followers of Jesus were not fasting. Jesus had never taught His disciples to fast, and so these followers of John the Baptist were confused about this. Why didn't the disciples of Jesus practice fasting? Jesus, seeing their confusion, explained to them, "The attendants of the bridegroom cannot mourn as long as the bridegroom is with them, can they? But the days will come when the bridegroom is taken away from them, and then they will fast" (Matthew 9:15). When Jesus was with the disciples, there was no need for mourning and fasting. The bridegroom was still with the wedding guests. The party was still going on. It was a time for joy, not sorrow; a time for feasting, not fasting. The idea of mourning was associated with seeking the Lord. They had no reason to seek the Lord—He was with them. It was a time of rejoicing, a time of happiness, a time of learning and growing. Jesus was saying, "I am with them; this is a glad time. They've got time enough to fast after I'm gone. Then they will fast; then they will seek Me." Today the bridegroom is gone. He will not return until His second coming, when He comes for His bride, the church. Between the time that He left us and the time He returns, Jesus says, the church will fast.

Now it seems to me that that's a pretty clear biblical teaching about fasting from Jesus Himself. Because the bridegroom is gone, the early church practiced prayer accompanied by fasting. Saul of Tarsus, after he met the Lord on the Damascus road, spent three days in an absolute complete fast of neither food nor water. Cornelius, in Acts 10, was fasting, waiting for Peter to come in response to the vision. It also is interesting to note that in Acts 13:2, 3, the church in Antioch fasted and prayed, "and while they were ministering to the Lord and fasting [this is the whole church], the Holy Spirit said, 'Set apart for Me Barnabus and Saul for the work to which I have called them.' Then, when they had fasted and prayed and laid their hands on them, they sent them away." The sending out of Paul and Barnabus to be the first missionaries was preceded by prayer and fasting in the early church. (Compare Acts 14:23: "And when they had appointed elders for them in every church, having prayed with fasting, they commended them to the Lord in whom they had believed.") After Paul and Barnabus went out and started preaching the gospel in Asia, they would come to a city, raise up a church, and then as they were leaving that church, they would appoint elders. How did they determine who were the elders they would leave behind?

They sought the Lord through prayer and *fasting*. Interesting, isn't it? All through the New Testament, the Bible teaches us to fast.

Different Kinds of Fasts

The Partial Fast. Now what kinds of fasts are there in the Bible? Let me list four different kinds of fasts that we find in the Scriptures. First, there is what I would call a partial fast. Daniel 10:3 describes a partial fast. Daniel says, "I did not eat any tasty food, nor did meat or wine enter my mouth." In other words, Daniel ate only vegetables in his partial fast. The partial fast is one in which the person would give up delicacies or some other item—that word *delicacies* literally means "cakes," or extras. So, if for spiritual reasons you were to go on a partial fast, maybe you would only eat one meal a day, or maybe you would give up certain things and only eat vegetables, as Daniel did. That would be a partial fast: when you eat some food, but in a limited, restricted diet. You do this because God has called you to do so.

The Popular Fast. The next step would be what we might call a "popular" fast. Because it's the most popular fast in the Bible, some people call it the normal fast. The normal fast would be one in which you give up food but you continue to drink water. That's the most common fast in the Scriptures, where one eats no food but continues to drink water or juices. This is what our Lord did in Matthew, chapter four, when He was forty days and forty nights fasting in the desert. The Bible says that after forty days and nights He became hungry. Did you notice it didn't say He became thirsty as well? And Satan tempted Him to turn the stone into bread, but Satan never tempted Him where thirst was concerned. Perhaps it is an argument from silence, but I assume our Lord practiced a normal fast, in that He had water during that forty days. If He did not have water, He had supernatural help from God to survive.

The Perfect Fast.   Now Moses, as I mentioned earlier, went on what we might call the perfect fast, or complete fast. The perfect fast would mean no food or water for a prescribed period of time. Moses would have died if God had not intervened: no one could do what Moses did without supernatural intervention. And here we have the longest fast in the Bible: two successive fasts of forty days—eighty days of fasting without food and water! There are many instances in the Bible where people experienced a complete fast for three days. It seems to be a significant time of fasting. Paul had a complete fast, a perfect fast, for three days—no food or water prior to his being baptized (*see* Acts 9:9). Ezra, too, sought the Lord by proclaiming a fast for the children of Israel. For three days and nights they fasted by the river Ahava. Ezra 8 records, "So we fasted and sought our God concerning this matter, and He listened to our entreaty" (Ezra 8:23). In Esther 4:16, Esther called her people the Jews to prayer and fasting, lest they be annihilated. As they were under threat of annihilation, she called her people to an absolute perfect fast of no food or water for three days, while she and her maidens did the same.

The Prolonged Fast.   Then there is what we might call the prolonged fast. The prolonged fast, of more than three days, is mentioned throughout the Bible. A fast of fifteen days, twenty days, or forty days is a long period of fasting. Personally, I have never fasted more than five days, but I have known many friends who have fasted for twenty days. I watched Arthur Blessitt, on Sunset Strip, drinking only water or fruit juice, fast for twenty-eight days. Later, in Washington, D.C., he fasted for forty days. This is the prolonged fast, normally drinking water only.

Those Who Fast

Is the practice of fasting only for the mystics or misfits of the church? Is there a place for it in every Christian's life? I think there is a place for fasting in my life. I believe God uses it in my own life. However, fasting is not commanded by God to the church today. He does *call* us to a ministry of prayer and intercession. This ministry will nearly always include fasting in order to discipline our spirit for the warfare at hand. In fact, I think 2 Chronicles 7:14, even though it doesn't mention fasting, is a call to prayer and mourning over our sin-sick nation: "If . . . My people who are called by My name humble themselves and pray. . . ." Notice, "humble themselves." Nothing humbles quite like fasting does. There may come a time when you have a great need to pray for someone, and you feel called of God for a certain purpose, for a certain need, to set aside a period of time to do without food or water. You will do this for spiritual reasons, for twenty-four hours or for some period of time, as God directs. Well, the question may be coming up in your mind, what are some definite spiritual reasons for fasting? Since fasting can have spiritual benefits, what are they?

Fasting to Seek God. In the Bible, the purpose of fasting is always spiritual. Scriptural fasting is always to seek God. From my own experience, I have learned that when God is leading me to fast and He calls me to fast for a specific reason, I have never had any trouble fasting. I have never gotten hungry, I've never had any trouble with it, and as I said, from time to time I have fasted for five days, and have never had any problem with it. However, when I decided I was going to fast without God's direction, wow! To me that is just like dieting. All I think about is food. I'd rather God call me to fast forty days than for me to try to diet, because all I do is think about food all day long. When fasting is a call from God, its purpose is always spiritual in nature, and it will be a great blessing to you. That's why the Bible talks about the fast that God shall choose, God's chosen fast (*see* Ezekiel 58). You are only to fast when God leads you to do so, and He will lead you to do so for spiritual reasons.

Fasting for Contrition. First, there is the fast of contrition. That is, fasting can be a tool to repentance, to humility, and to seeking God. It has a tremendous power to humble our spirit.

It's an aid to spiritual discipline. It can be an aid to repentance and seeking the Lord. Let me give some verses from David in the Psalms. In Psalms 35:13, David said, "I humbled my soul with fasting." Did you hear that? Again, David said, "when I wept in my soul with fasting" (Psalms 69:10). Ezra tells the people they will declare a fast by the river of Ahava in order to humble their souls before the Lord (*see* Ezra 8:21).

John Wesley and Fasting. Fasting to humble the spirit has been practiced by nearly all of God's special servants. One of my heroes of the faith is John Wesley. In Wesley's famous sermon on fasting he concludes:

> First, let it be done unto the Lord, with our eye singly fixed on Him. Let our intention herein be this, and this alone, to glorify our Father which is in heaven; to express our sorrow and shame for our manifold transgressions of His holy law; to wait for an increase of purifying grace, drawing our affections to things above; to add seriousness and earnestness to our prayers; to avert the wrath of God; and to obtain all the great and precious promises which He hath made to us in Jesus Christ.... Let us beware of fancying we *merit* anything of God by our fasting. We cannot be too often warned of this; inasmuch as a desire to "establish our own righteousness," to procure salvation of debt and not of grace, is so deeply rooted in all our hearts. Fasting is only a way which God hath ordained, wherein we wait for His unmerited mercy; and wherein, without any desert of ours, He hath promised freely to give us His blessing.[1]

God calls us to fast to humble us, that we may seek His Holy face. Fasting is for us *and* for Him. Every thought of food is a call to pray, to seek God. Fasting shows us the frailty of our life. We are dependent creatures. We must have daily bread to survive. Fasting humbles the soul; it reminds us that we are dust and only God is our source. Fasting can break the bonds of the flesh and free the spirit to soar with God.

Fasting can do away with pride. I think it is interesting how many times the Bible talks about how when "their bellies were full," they committed adultery. The Bible says that the people of Sodom fed their bellies full with eating and drinking and then they went off into sexual sin. They became proud in their hearts—and it's interesting to see how, when people are physically fat in the sense of being overindulgent, pride becomes associated with such affluence. In the Bible, fasting has to do with humbling because it can make a proud spirit contrite before God, and it can free the soul to seek the Lord as the body is disciplined and mastery is gained over it.

Fasting can be a part of mourning. In Matthew 5:4, Jesus talked about how blessed are they that mourn, for they shall be comforted. I think it's interesting that in Matthew 9:15, the words *mourning* and *fasting* are almost interchangeable in the thinking of Jesus. Mourning is almost interchangeable with fasting, and so it has the ability to humble our spirit before God.

Consecration. Also, fasting may be for consecration. Have you ever had a time in your life when you wanted to see the Lord? You just desperately needed a closer walk with God, and you needed to know more of Him, to know more of His Word? Did you know that throughout the Bible, fasting is associated with seeking the Lord, with consecration, and setting yourself apart for God? Why do you think Jesus went into the wilderness for forty days? It was just prior to His public ministry, was it not? And so Jesus fasted, that He might seek the Lord for His life and for His ministry. Fasting is many times given to a Christian just prior to some great calling or some great task in order to seek an in-filling of the Holy Spirit. To seek the Lord for consecration and for ministry—that's what we have in Acts 13 when they set aside Paul and Barnabus to send them out as church missionaries. The church prayed and fasted; then they laid hands on Paul and Barnabus to send them out, dedicated to Christ.

Fasting can also be associated with seeking a revelation from God. Maybe you are just trying to find God's will on a certain matter, and you don't know what God wants you to do. The Bible gives illustration where you can seek the Lord through prayer and fasting, to just completely give yourself to God—spirit, soul, and body—so that every thought is brought captive to God. You see, when you fast, it is unto the Lord. In Acts 13:2, it says the church was fasting unto the Lord. You don't fast for your own benefit. Too many times as Christians we ask the question, what can I get out of this? Why should I fast; what can I get out of this? Listen, fasting is unto the Lord. It says of Anna, the prophetess, in Luke 2, that she was worshiping with fasting. Have you ever done that? Very few believers have ever done that. Worshiping with fasting: it's an act of worship in which you seek God with your total being.

We've seen the fast of contrition and the fast of consecration. Now let's look at the fast of concern, the fast of concern for others.

Fast of Concern.   You see, fasting is associated throughout the Bible with praying for others. Let's talk about prayer and fasting. Fasting is never to be an end in itself. Nowhere in the Bible are you to fast just for the sake of fasting. Fasting is always linked with some other purpose and some other goal. For instance, the Bible talks about praying and fasting, watching and fasting, worshiping and fasting, seeking the Lord and fasting. Fasting is always associated with something else; and it is closely linked with prayer because, you see, fasting creates in the Christian an atmosphere for praying, for reading the Word of God, and for seeking the Lord. It literally frees the soul to seek God. Now this has been proven scientifically—that when people are in a fasting condition, their minds have greater alertness, their eyes have a greater sparkle. Your mind is just more alert when you're fasting than any other time. It seems as though when the body is subdued and is being cleansed, that your spirit is freed to pray and to understand spiritual truths. I want you to know that I have received some of the greatest truth from God's Word in periods of prayer and fasting. God's Word has just literally come alive to me, and prayer and fellowship with God have become dearer to me than any other time, through prayer and fasting.

Prayer and Fasting

Now, let me just list three areas where fasting is linked with prayer.

Fasting and Intercession. Fasting and prayer can be for intercession, for praying for others. That's what we have in the book of Esther, where Esther called her people to pray for the Jews that they might not be annihilated by the king. And through prayer and fasting they were praying for the nation. This is what we have again in the passage in Ezra 8 that I mentioned earlier: God's people praying, humbling their souls, that He might spare their nation. Do you remember the story of Jonah and Ninevah, where the king of Ninevah called the city of Ninevah to national prayer and fasting, so that God would not destroy them? All through the Bible, fasting and prayer is associated with intercession, praying for others.

Fasting and Revival. As I travel from place to place, I keep hearing churches and preachers talk about revival. Oh, how we need revival in our churches; how we need revival in America! America will never experience revival—you will never personally experience revival—without fasting. All through the Bible, revival and renewal are associated with prayer and fasting. You show me a church that gets desperate for God; you show me a Christian who gets a God-hunger, who will hunger and

thirst after God so desperately that he seeks the Lord to the
point that he has no need for food because he is so desperate
to seek Him—then I tell you, God will honor that Christian,
that church. Prayer and fasting is linked with revival, it is *intimately* linked with revival. I think Satan has blinded our eyes
to this tremendous spiritual avenue for gaining access to
God.

Fasting and Deliverance.   Prayer and fasting may also be offered for deliverance. Prayer and fasting is for deliverance of
other people. I only want to mention these, but all through the
Bible the Bible says that we can deliver other people from
bondage through prayer and fasting. Now what kind of deliverance are we talking about? In Deuteronomy, Moses prayed
for the nation of Israel. Listen to what Moses prayed; he says,
"I fell down before the Lord, as at the first, forty days and
nights; I neither ate bread nor drank water, because of all your
sin which you had committed . . ." (Deuteronomy 9:18). Moses
fasted for someone else. He stood in the gap, an intercessor,
literally laying his life down for the nation Israel. His intercession delivered an entire nation! We today can also stand in the
gap for those in bondage. You know people who are sick—
physically, emotionally, and spiritually. They need deliverance; especially those who are sick because of sin. The alco-
holic, drug addict, or those who are spiritually oppressed
because of sin: these in bondage need to be set free. How can
they be liberated?

Matthew Seventeen.   A great lesson on prayer and fasting is
taught in Matthew 17:14–21. A man's son was "moonsmitten"
(as the Greek reads). The boy was continually having seizures
and would throw himself into the fire or water, trying to kill
himself. The disciples knew his problem to be demonic. Satan
was trying to kill this boy. The disciples tried to set the boy free
but were powerless against the demons that possessed him. The
father comes to our Lord and tells of the disciples' failure.

Jesus has the boy brought forward and commands the demon to release the boy; he is delivered immediately. The disciples later come to Jesus privately and ask, "Why could we not cast it out?" Jesus then rebukes His disciples by saying, "Because of the littleness of your faith; for truly I say to you, if you have faith as a mustard seed, you shall say to this mountain, 'Move from here to there,' and it shall move; and nothing shall be impossible to you. But this kind does not go out except by prayer and fasting" (Matthew 17:20, 21).

Jesus would have us know that those in any kind of spiritual bondage can be set free. All that is required is for someone with faith to stand in the gap for that person. An intercessor who will fast and pray until the victory is won is all that is required. Andrew Murray, commenting on this passage, says, "Faith needs prayer for its full growth. And prayer needs fasting for its full growth . . . Prayer is the one hand with which we grasp the invisible; fasting, the other, with which we let loose and cast away the visible."[2] You see, Satan will resist us. He is not easily defeated. It is the church's task to "bring every thought captive to Christ," and to tear down Satan's strongholds (*see* 2 Corinthians 10:4, 5). Prayer alone is many times not enough. Fasting and prayer adds more than our words on the line—it lays down the life. It says to God and to the enemy, "I will not eat 'til the battle is won." Fasting is a prayer without words. It is the intercessor's statement of resolve. Arthur Wallis, in his wonderful book *God's Chosen Fast,* quotes Andrew Murray: "Fasting is, before God, a practical proof that the thing we ask is to us a matter of true and pressing interest, and inasmuch as in a high degree it strengthens the intensity and power of prayer, and becomes the unceasing practical expression of a prayer without words. . . ."[3]

When You Fast

Dear reader, it is my prayer for you that, as you have read these teachings on prayer and fasting, you have come to see that for you, as a follower of Christ, the issue is not *"if"* you should fast, but rather *"when"* you fast.

May I suggest that you simply determine to set aside a twenty-four hour period, perhaps from noon to noon? The body grows accustomed to fasting by degrees. During a brief twenty-four-hour fast, your body will experience no real hunger—only psychological hunger. The stomach may "growl" because it is a crybaby accustomed to being fed at regular intervals. During the times you think of food, use these moments as a call to prayer; a time to seek God. Determine to fast "unto the Lord." Use this time to dedicate yourself to Him. It is best that you have a definite goal or purpose for fasting. It may be for contrition, consecration, or for intercession. I personally often find myself fasting primarily to pray and stand in the gap for others. Often, I'll fast and pray for a country, or for a Christian in ministry that I know in Romania, Poland, the Philippines, and so on.

Now, as you begin, should your fast be complete or partial? You may decide on a complete fast—no food or water. That's between you and God. Perhaps, you are fearful, anxious, or uncertain that you can do this. Be assured: when your Heavenly Father calls you to fast, He will sustain you, bless you, and thrill you with His presence. The joy of the Lord will be your strength. Food will become unattractive to you. Those who desire to truly be prayer warriors must "break through" onto holy ground. Fasting then becomes as natural as a soldier loading his rifle. It is a weapon we use and welcome.

> Grant us the will to fashion as we feel,
> Grant us the strength to labour as we know,
> Grant us the purpose, ribbed and edged with steel,
> To strike the blow.

> John Drinkwater[4]

Resources

1. John Wesley, quoted in Arthur Wallis, *God's Chosen Fast* (Fort Washington, Pennsylvania: Christian Literature Crusade, Inc., 1968), pp. 34, 35.

2. Andrew Murray, *With Christ in the School of Prayer* (Old Tappan, New Jersey: Fleming H. Revell Company, 1965), p. 74.

3. Wallis, *God's Chosen Fast*, p. 55.

4. Quoted in Wallis, p. 84.

Additional Reading

Bounds, E. M. *Power Through Prayer*. Springdale, Pennsylvania: Whitaker House, 1983.

—— *A Treasury of Prayer*. Minneapolis: Bethany House, 1981.

Chadwick, Samuel. *The Path of Prayer*. Fort Washington, Pennsylvania: Christian Literature Crusade, Inc., 1963.

Gordon, S. D. *Quiet Talks on Prayer*. Grand Rapids, Michigan: Baker Book House, 1980.

Grubb, Norman. *Rees Howells, Intercessor*. Fort Washington, Pennsylvania: Christian Literature Crusade, Inc., 1964–1967.

Hallesby, O. *Prayer*. Minneapolis: Augsburg Publishing House, 1975.

Hayford, Jack. *Prayer Is Invading the Impossible*. South Plainfield, New Jersey: Bridge Publishing Company, 1977.

Huegel, F. J. *The Ministry of Intercession*. Minneapolis: Bethany House, 1971.

The Kneeling Christian. Grand Rapids, Michigan: Zondervan Publishing House, 1979.

Miller, Basil. *George Muller: Man of Faith*. Minneapolis: Bethany House, 1972.

M'Intyre, David M. *The Hidden Life of Prayer*. Grand Rapids, Michigan: Baker Book House, 1979.

Morgan, G. Campbell. *The Practice of Prayer* (Morgan Library). Grand Rapids, Michigan: Baker Book House.

Murray, Andrew. *Helps to Intercession*. Fort Washington, Pennsylvania: Christian Literature Crusade, Inc., 1965.

—— *The Ministry of Intercession.* Old Tappan, New Jersey: Fleming H. Revell Company, 1952.

—— *The Power of the Blood.* Fort Washington, Pennsylvania: Christian Literature Crusade, Inc., 1965.

—— *With Christ in the School of Prayer.* Springdale, Pennsylvania: Whitaker House, 1981.

Parker, William R. *Prayer Can Change Your Life.* New York: Cornerstone, 1974.

Prince, Derek. *Shaping History Through Prayer and Fasting.* Fort Lauderdale, Florida: Derek Prince Ministries Publications, 1973.

Rinker, Rosalind. *Conversational Prayer.* Waco, Texas: Word Books, 1976.

—— *Prayer: Conversing With God.* Grand Rapids, Michigan: Zondervan Publishing House, 1959.

Sanders, J. Oswald. *Effective Prayer.* Robesonia, Pennsylvania: OMF Books, 1961.

Searle, Walter. *David Brainerd's Personal Testimony.* Grand Rapids, Michigan: Baker Book House, 1979.

Simpson, A. B. *The Life of Prayer.* Harrisburg, Pennsylvania: Christian Publications, 1975.

Torrey, R. A. *How to Pray.* Chicago: Moody Press.

Wallis, Arthur. *God's Chosen Fast.* Fort Washington, Pennsylvania: Christian Literature Crusade, Inc., 1970.

—— *Pray in the Spirit.* Fort Washington, Pennsylvania: Christian Literature Crusade, Inc., 1970.